IMAGES
of America

SCOTLAND
COUNTY

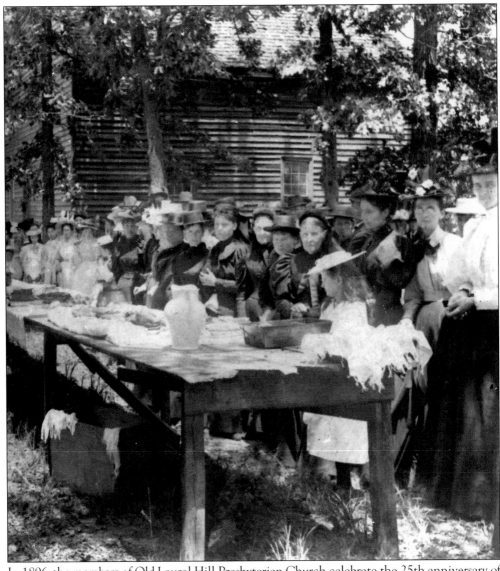

In 1896, the members of Old Laurel Hill Presbyterian Church celebrate the 25th anniversary of Rev. Angus Ferguson's pastorate. (Courtesy of Margaret Pittman.)

IMAGES
of America

SCOTLAND
COUNTY

John D. Stewart, Sara Stewart,
and the Historic Properties Commission

ARCADIA
PUBLISHING

Published by Arcadia Publishing
Charleston, South Carolina

Printed in the United States of America

Library of Congress Catalog Card Number: 2001090009

For all general information contact Arcadia Publishing at:
Telephone 843-853-2070
Fax 843-853-0044
E-mail sales@arcadiapublishing.com
For customer service and orders:
Toll-Free 1-888-313-2665

Visit us on the Internet at www.arcadiapublishing.com

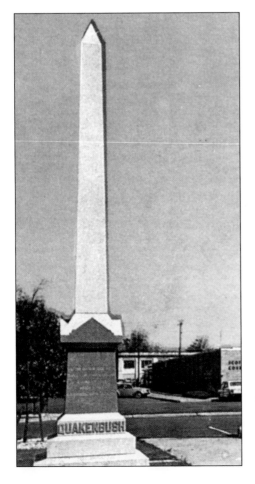

The Quackenbush Monument, the only monument in North Carolina erected to honor a schoolteacher, stands in front of the Scotland County Courthouse. (Courtesy of Isabella Bostick.)

CONTENTS

ACKNOWLEDGMENTS

Scotland County has been a labor of love and cooperation for all of the people of Scotland County. We want to thank Clyde Marsh who opened the drawer of old photos at *The Laurinburg Exchange* office to us when we first started, giving us the assurance that we could find 200 interesting pictures. Thanks also to the Parks and Recreation Department for letting us use the old pictures at the John Blue House and to Lucy Walters for sharing pictures of the Gill family from the Gill House. Both of these houses are property of Historic Properties.

We also want to thank all of the citizens of Scotland County who shared part of their histories with us. We are trying to show insight into the lives of Scotland County people, some famous and some infamous. Each of you has reminded us of what a great place Scotland County is in which to live.

The history of an area is not just about big news items or famous people. Everyday life is just as much history as unusual happenings, and we want this book to show as much as possible of both. We tried to include all of the people we could as well, and we hope you enjoy your history.

The proceeds from the sale of this book will go to the Scotland County Historic Properties Commission. The money will help with the maintenance and upkeep the properties that are owned by the commission.

—John and Sara Stewart

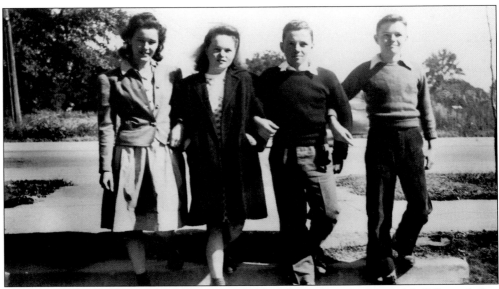

Four good friends—Katherine Thompson, Betty Summerlin, Gramling McGill, and Ray Jones—walk around town in the 1940s.

INTRODUCTION

As early as 1729, there were settlers in the area in and around what is now known as Scotland County, North Carolina. The main influx came just after the Revolutionary War. A large group of people from the Highlands of Scotland came up from the Cape Fear and settled in two parts of the county, which was at that time part of Bladen County. One group settled in the northern part of the county, near Old Laurel Hill Church, and another group settled in the John's area. Both groups appear to have been from the same general area in Scotland. Later, other European groups, including Germans, Welsh, English, and Ulster Scots settled in the area. There were also people from countries in Africa, most of whom did not come of their own volition.

Before this, however, Native Americans populated the area. They seemed to have been accepting of the immigrants as no evidence of animosity has been found.

As the population in North Carolina increased, the counties began to split up into smaller areas. Today's Scotland County was separated from Bladen County and was part of Anson County. When Anson divided, it became a part of Richmond County. By the end of the Civil War, a group decided to try to split the area from Richmond to become its own county. After several appeals, the state granted the group permission, and in 1899, Scotland County became a county all its own.

Many interesting sites lie within the county. Included is the oldest church in the area, Laurel Hill Presbyterian Church, which was founded in 1797 and is still in existence. Another interesting site is Stewartsville Cemetery, which is the resting place of early Scottish settlers, African Americans, and Native Americans who were all residents of the county. A nearby sign erected by the state marks the cemetery as an important historical site.

After a century of being an agricultural area, the county began to grow industrially after 1950. Scotland County is now the home to a variety of industries that create different types of products. There are also several international companies that produce materials in the county. For the centennial celebration, the motto shows the way in which citizens feel about themselves and their county—"Proud Past; Vibrant Present; Progressive Future."

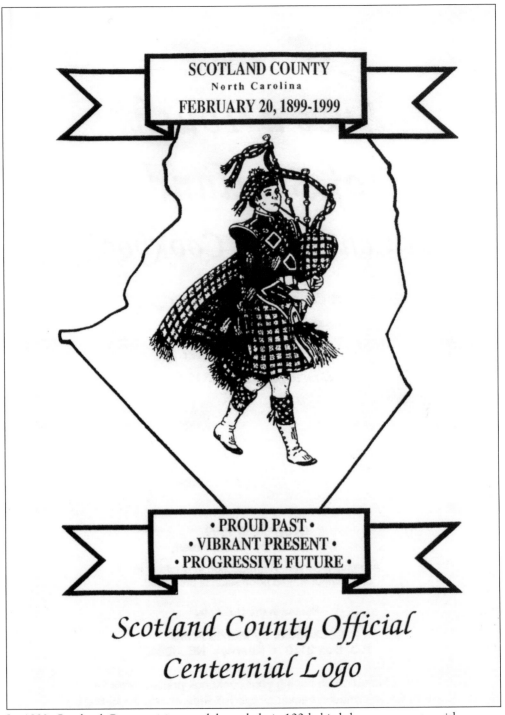

SCOTLAND COUNTY

North Carolina

FEBRUARY 20, 1899-1999

• PROUD PAST •
• VIBRANT PRESENT •
• PROGRESSIVE FUTURE •

Scotland County Official Centennial Logo

In 1999, Scotland County citizens celebrated their 100th birthday as a county with a year-long party. Something special was held in every month of the year. An attempt was made to include each part of the county and all of its residents. Shown is the official logo for the county's centennial year. (Courtesy of the Scotland County Centennial Committee.)

One

PEOPLE

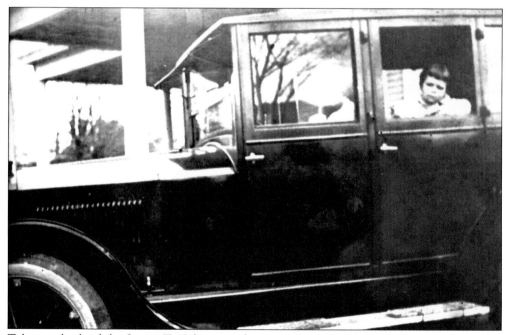

Taken in back of the Jasper T. Gibson residence on East Church Street in Laurinburg, this picture shows the family sedan in about 1920 with daughter Doris in the back seat. (Courtesy Reg and Marilyn McVicker.)

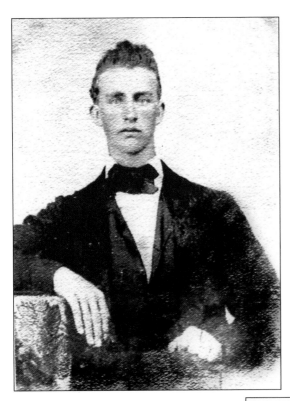

Jehu Thomas Gibson, born in Richmond County, North Carolina in 1840, volunteered and joined Co. A 5th Battalion, light infantry, C.S.A. where he attained the rank of sergeant. He married Frances Ann Lovin in January 1867. (Courtesy of Reg and Marilyn McVicker.)

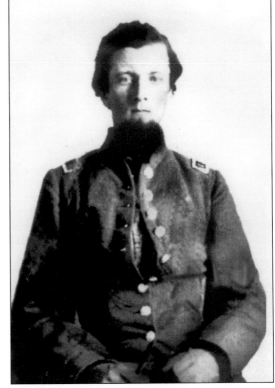

Jesse Hargrave was a captain in Co. 1 of the 14th. division, C.S.A. in the Civil War. He was from Scotland County and returned here after the war. (Courtesy of Jack Matthews.)

Sam Dunlap was the sheriff at Wagram in 1912. Before that he had been sheriff in Maxton, where he apprehended a notorious outlaw. (Courtesy of Sylvia McLean.)

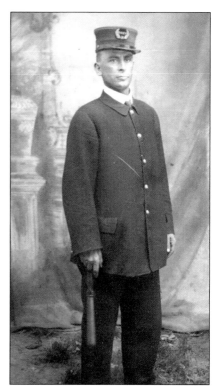

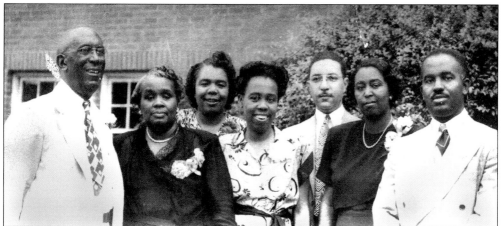

African-American citizens of Scotland County wrote to Dr. Booker T. Washington in 1903 requesting that he send teachers to start a school in the county. Basic elementary education was all that the state provided at that time, and locals felt they could get better jobs with more education. Dr. Washington sent newlyweds Emanuel and Tinny McDuffie, who hitched train rides to get there. He was 18 and she was 17 when they arrived, and they had about $1 between them. However, they were able to raise money from the local sharecroppers and appealed to one of the founding fathers of Laurinburg. They were able to buy some swamp land where they built a log classroom after draining the land with the help of the local black population. Shown here are Mr. E.M. McDuffie, Mrs. E.M. McDuffie, Ms. V.T. Efferson, Ms. Musa Butler, J.C. Melton, Ida Melton, and R.S. McDuffie, who were the faculty of the school in 1946. (Courtesy of Bishop McDuffie.)

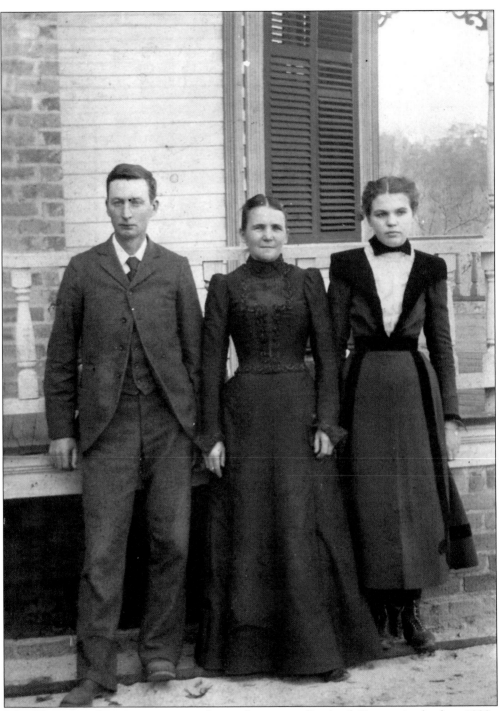

John Blue was a farmer, inventor, and manufacturer in Scotland County in the late 1800s. He built the Victorian John Blue house in 1880s and is pictured with his wife Flora Jane McKinnon and his daughter Edna Earl. Edna married Edward S. Rudd and had a daughter, Edna Blue. She married John Gilchrist Purcell and presently resides at Scotia Village. (Courtesy of John Blue House.)

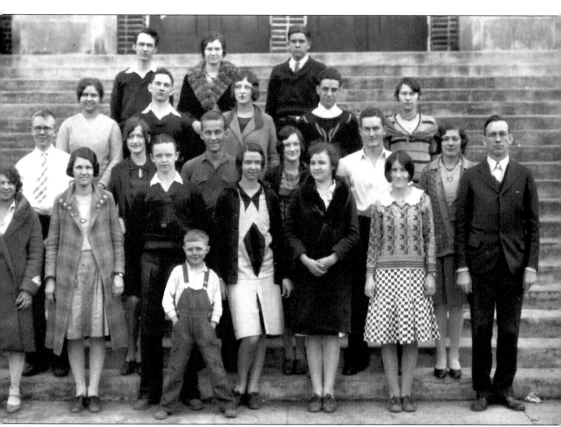

Mr. Kiser taught this tenth grade class at Laurinburg High School in 1929. He became principal and later was a member of the North Carolina House of Representatives, where he served for many years. (Courtesy of Reg and Marilyn McVicker.)

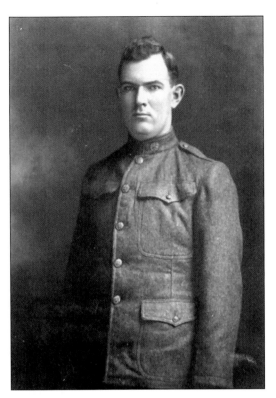

John Davis McLean, pictured here in his military uniform, was one of many Scotland County men who served in World War I. (Courtesy of Sylvia McLean.)

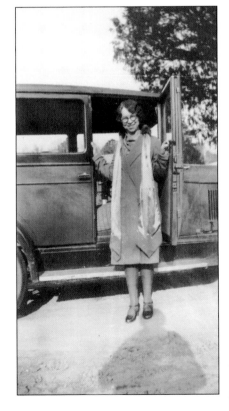

Miss Thelma Gibson, who graduated from Women's College of the University of North Carolina in Greensboro and taught school for many years, is shown with her new "flivver" in the 1920s. She later retired and moved back home to Scotland County. (Courtesy of Millie Yongue.)

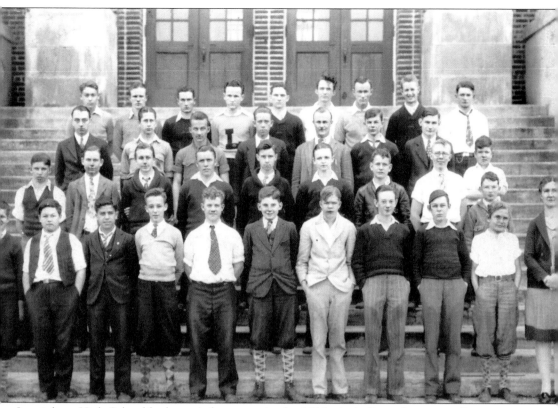

Laurinburg High School had a varied program in the 1930s, including a focus on college prep and cultural arts. Pictured is the boys' glee club. (Courtesy of Reg and Marilyn McVicker.)

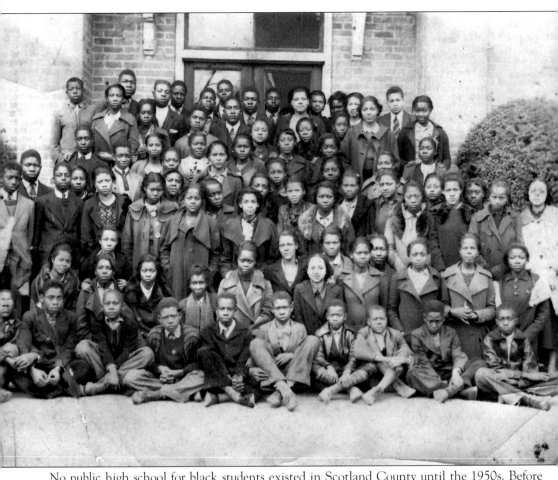

No public high school for black students existed in Scotland County until the 1950s. Before that, they were educated at the Laurinburg Institute, a private school. Local students were allowed to go as day students. Shown is the ninth grade class, pictured in 1939. Two class members were Helen Ware and Needham Gee. (Courtesy of Myrtle Ware.)

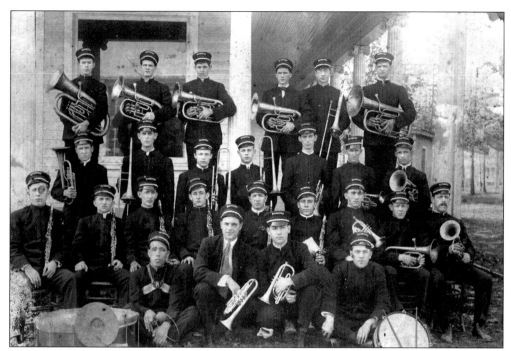

In the early part of the 20th century, Scotland County was home to several cultural organizations, including an opera house. The band pictured here played in Laurinburg and was organized in the early 1900s. (Courtesy of *The Laurinburg Exchange*.)

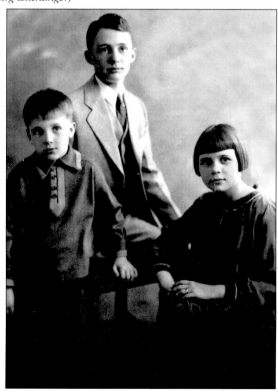

Ralph, Tom, and Doris Gibson pose for a portrait in the 1920s. They were children of Mr. and Mrs. J.T. Gibson of Laurinburg. (Courtesy of Reg and Marilyn McVicker.)

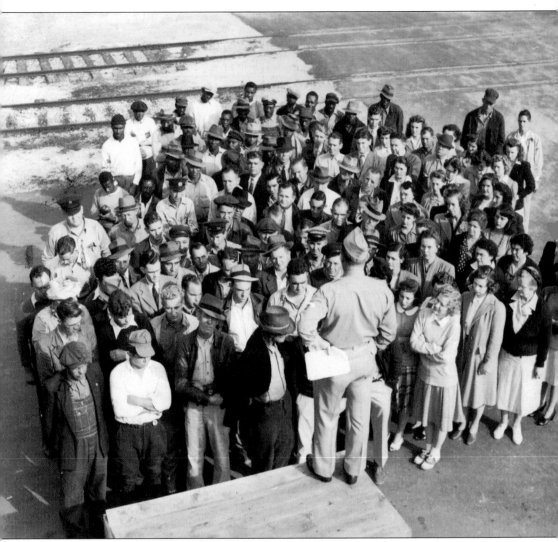

Many of these people were from Scotland County and were the civilian employees at Laurinburg-Maxton Airbase. The base was in the eastern corner of Scotland County during World War II, and it was established to train glider pilots for the war. The base provided many well-paying jobs for the local population. (Courtesy of Margaret Pittman.)

Myrtle Ware was born in the Hasty section of Scotland County. She graduated from Laurinburg Institute and Fayetteville State College and taught first grade in several parts of the state before returning home. She was an excellent teacher who was loved by her students. (Courtesy of Myrtle Ware.)

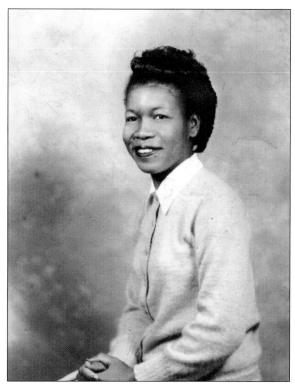

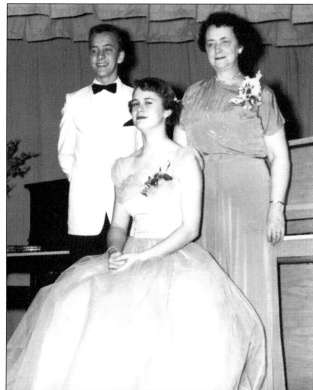

Mrs. R.E. Yongue was a long-time organist at First United Methodist Church and taught piano to many young people of Scotland County. Two of her pupils, Jack Peacock and Jeanne Aycock, are shown with their teacher. Both of these young people were winners of piano contests and were able to have an individual recital in the 1950s. (Courtesy of Millie Yongue.)

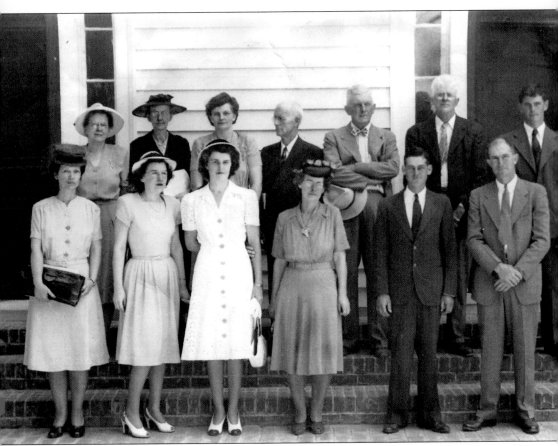

The leaders of Laurel Hill Presbyterian Church in 1940, shown here from left to right, are (front row) Miss Nellie McGirt, Mrs. Frances Murray, Mrs. Nan Godfrey, Mrs. Fannie Jackson, Bill Newton, and Eli Murray; (back row) Mrs. Liza Shaw, Mrs. Alma Alford, Mrs. Mary Newton, Mr. Fairley Murray, Mr. Raymond Monroe, Mr. Ralph Currie, and Marion Monroe. (Courtesy of Sylvia McLean.)

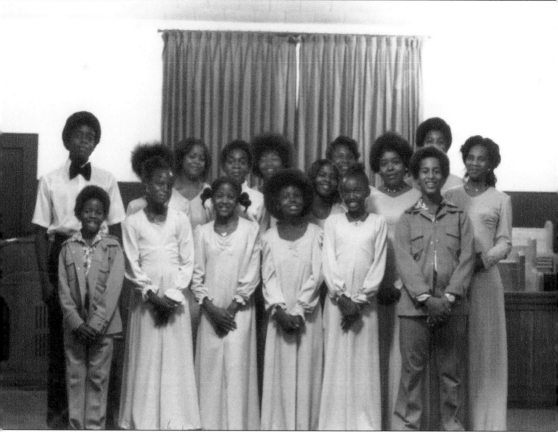

The gospel choir of the Spring Branch Missionary Baptist Church in Wagram are pictured here in 1974 and are identified, from left to right, as follows: (front row) Darren Gilchrist, Vaunzell Wells, Beverly Massey, Lisa Capel, Lorrain Wells, and John Gilchrist Jr.; (back row) Reginald Massey, Winona Massey, Queen Long, Edwell Gilchrist, Brenda Gilchrist, Coronelia Gilchrist, Ann Massey, and Maude Wells. (Courtesy of Maude Wells.)

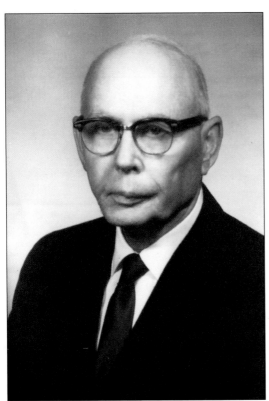

Thomas J. Gill was the first county auditor of Scotland County, and he held the job for many years. (Courtesy of *The Laurinburg Exchange*.)

Dr. Ansley Moore was the first president of St. Andrews Presbyterian College. He is pictured with Dr. William Friday (right), chancellor of the University of North Carolina. The picture was taken in the first year of St. Andrews, 1961. (Courtesy of St. Andrews College Archives.)

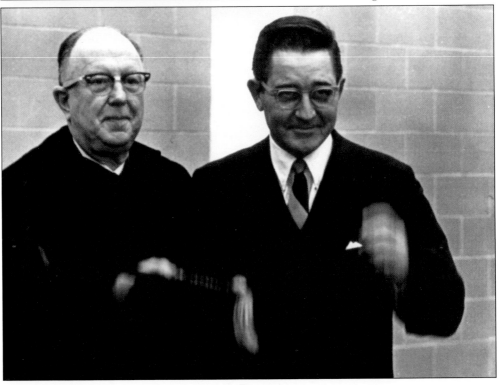

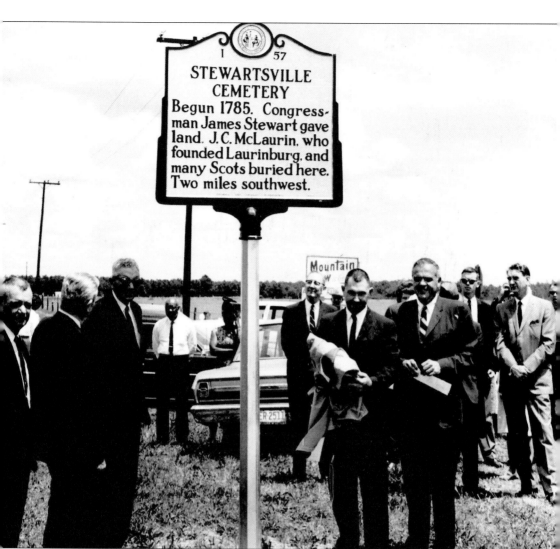

Stewartsville Cemetery, south of Laurinburg, was honored with a highway historical site marker in 1968. Here, John Carmichael, representing the Stewartsville Cemetery Association, helps unveil the sign on U.S. 74 in the eastern part of the county. (Courtesy of *The Laurinburg Exchange*.)

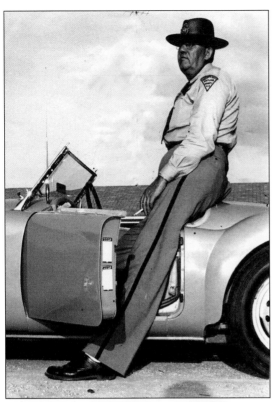

Deputy Sheriff Dusty Odom poses with a small sports car in 1970. He was a big man and the photographer wanted to contrast the size of the little car with Dusty's height. (Courtesy of Mary Odom.)

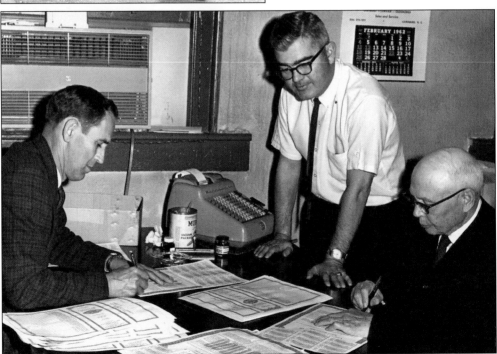

Sidney Smith, county commissioner, and Tom Gill, county auditor, sign school bonds as county attorney Walter Cashwell Jr. looks on. (Courtesy of *The Laurinburg Exchange*.)

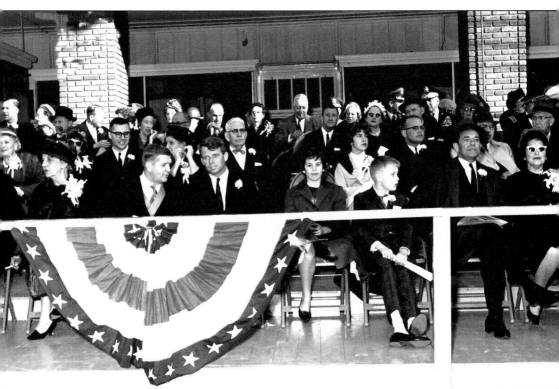

The governor of North Carolina from 1960 to 1964 was Terry Sanford, a Scotland County native. He was known as the "education governor" because during his term a sales tax was enacted to improve education in North Carolina. Governor Sanford was later a U.S. Senator and president of Duke University. Here, he is pictured at his inauguration in 1960. Famous people also shown are former Governor Hodges and Bobby Kennedy. Governor Sanford's mother, father, wife, and children are here, too. (Courtesy of *The Laurinburg Exchange*.)

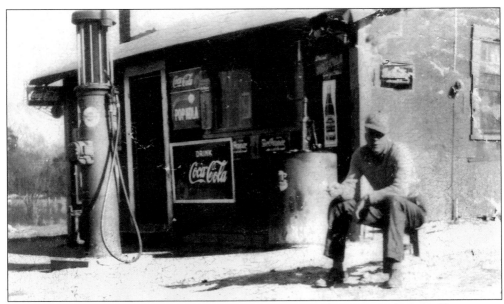

Mr. Willie Tyner operated a filling station in Springfield in the 1930s and 1940s. He is sitting in front of his store in 1945. (Courtesy Dolores Baxley.)

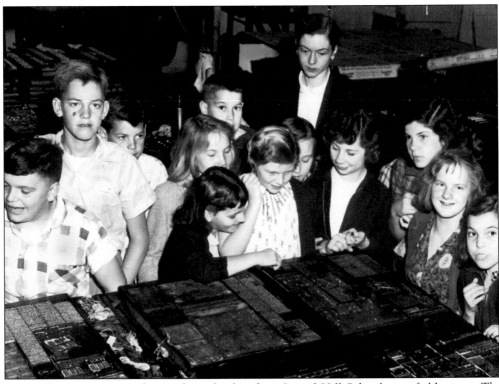

Mary Odom accompanies her sixth-grade class from Laurel Hill School on a field trip to *The Laurinburg Exchange* office in 1954. They were studying methods of communication. Mary was later a state senator. (Courtesy of *The Laurinburg Exchange*.)

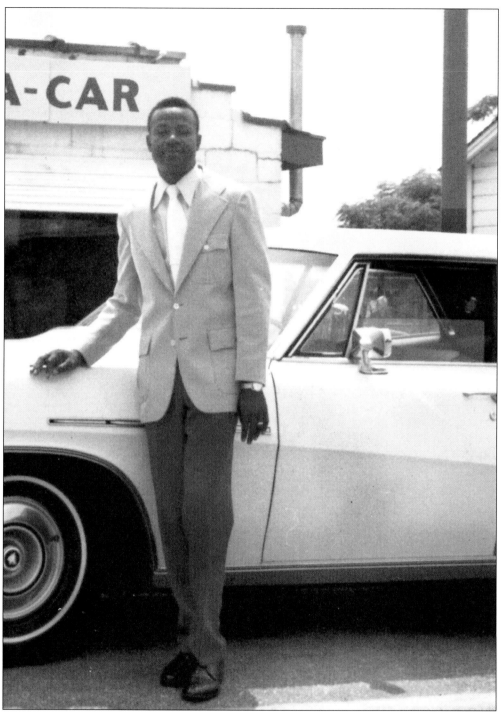

Rev. James McLean opened an automobile dealership in 1955 and was the first African-American auto dealer in Scotland County. He is pictured here in the 1970s. McLean is currently the minister of Star of Bethlehem Baptist Church. (Courtesy of Hazel McLean.)

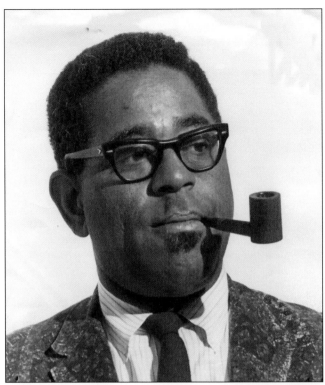

Dizzy Gillespie, a world-famous trumpeter, was born in nearby Cheraw, South Carolina. He went to school at the Laurinburg Institute, which was established in the early 1900s and provided high school education for the black population of Scotland and surrounding counties. (Courtesy of *The Laurinburg Exchange*.)

U.S. Senator and former governor Terry Sanford is greeted by Melody Hunter, Pam Ansley, and Will Whitehead on a visit to his home town in 1980, during the time that Laurinburg was nominated for the third time as an All America City. (Courtesy of Mutt McCoy.)

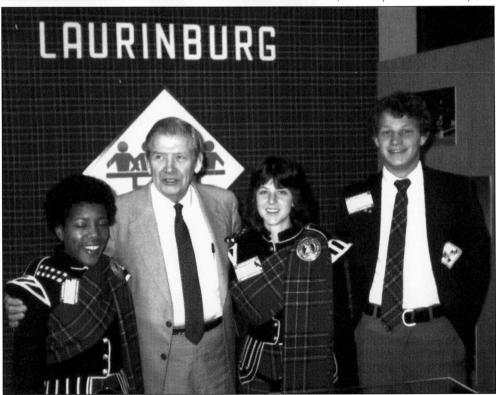

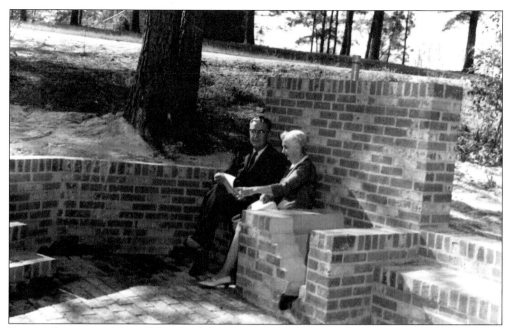

Former Superintendent of Scotland County Schools A.B. Gibson sits with Belle McNeill Monroe at the old spring on the grounds of Temperance Hall near Wagram. This picture was made in the 1950s. (Courtesy of *The Laurinburg Exchange*.)

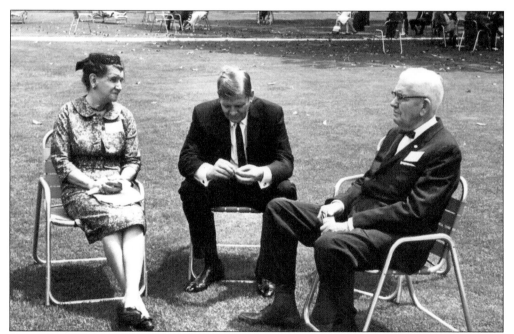

Governor Terry Sanford was born and reared in Laurinburg. His mother, who came from Virginia as a young teacher and married Mr. Cecil Sanford, was an esteemed educator in the county schools. Governor Sanford is pictured with his mother and father at a conference in Pinehurst in the 1960s. (Courtesy of John G. Hemmer and *The Laurinburg Exchange*.)

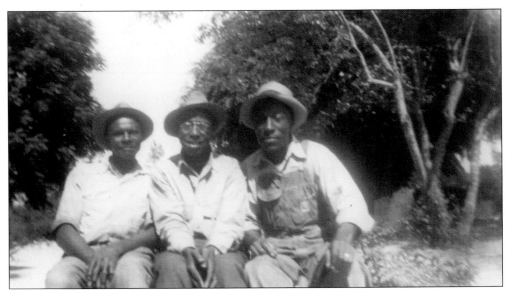

Mr. James Ware was a farmer in the Hasty section of Scotland County. Here he is seen with two lifelong friends, Will Leggett and Cario McLucas, in 1944. Mr. McLucas was the father of 21 children. (Courtesy Myrtle Ware.)

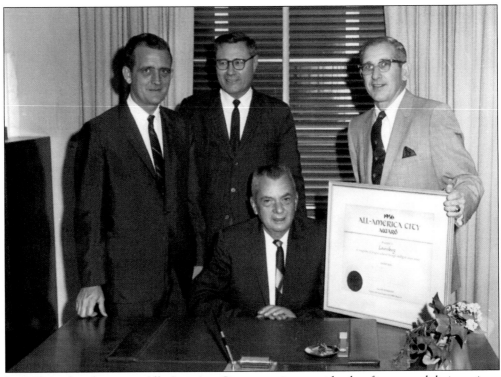

Laurinburg has been an All America City two times, with the first award being given in 1956. Here, Jim Milligan, Charles Wentz, and Wade Dunbar Jr. join with Mayor Dike Lytch to announce the first award. The second award was in 1967. (Courtesy of *The Laurinburg Exchange*.)

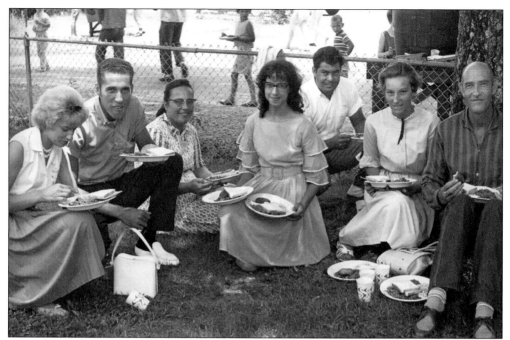

James Clark and his family enjoy their barbecue dinner under an oak tree in front of Waverly Mills Office on the Fourth of July in 1957. Mr. Clark was a twister hand at Prince Plant of Waverly Mills and had worked for the company for many years. (Courtesy *The Laurinburg Exchange*.)

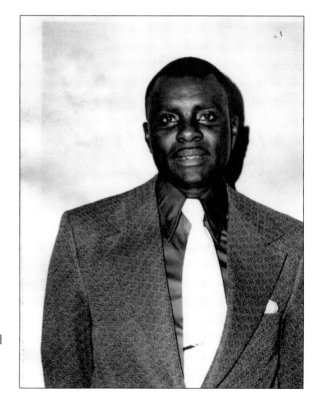

James Stewart was a native and life-long resident of Scotland County. He was a member of the city council and worked in personnel at Libby-Owens Ford. Mr. Stewart died in April 2001. (Courtesy of *The Laurinburg Exchange*.)

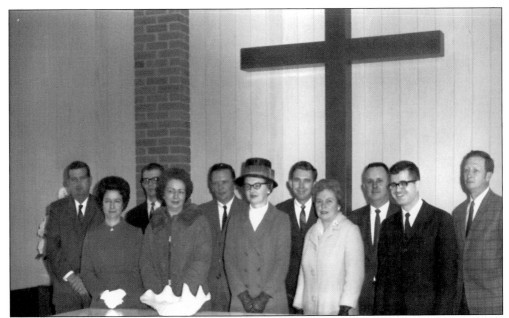

Members of the first building committee of St. Luke United Methodist Church, organized in 1969, were (from left to right) Ted Teal, Ann Braswell, Charles "Scoofer" Jordan, Evelyn Davis, F.L. Matheny, Susan King Combs, Don Ballard, Mary Harvin, Ned Barringer, Rev. Robert Pullman (church minister), and Charles Cox. (Courtesy of Rev. Bill Wells.)

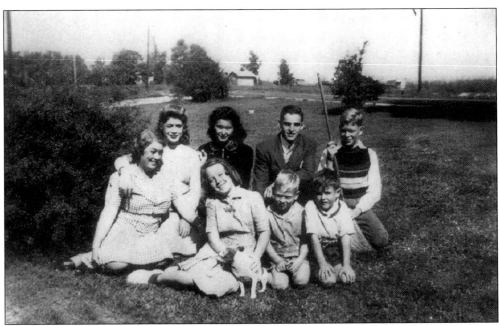

A happy family group enjoys each other and friends who are visiting in 1942. They are, from left to right, (front row) Emma Lee Myers, Katherine Stewart, John Stewart, and John McRae; (back row) Martha Stewart, Katherine Thompson, Jack Summerlin, and Angus Stewart. (Courtesy of Bobby Knotts.)

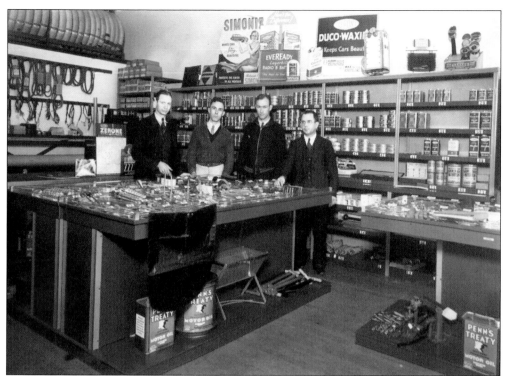

John Allred, Fred Thompson, Ed McLaurin, and Floyd McLean are standing in the McLean Supply Company—which sold auto parts and materials for repairing cars—in 1934. (Courtesy of Elsworth Stubbs.)

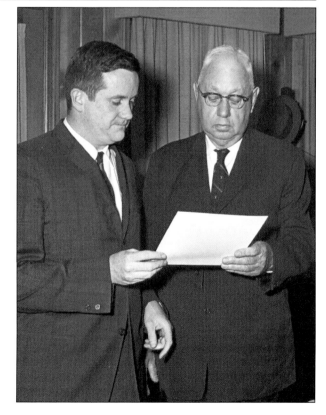

McNair Evans and R.E. Yongue look at the award given to Mr. Yongue from the Cotton Ginners of America in 1965. (Courtesy of Millie Yongue.)

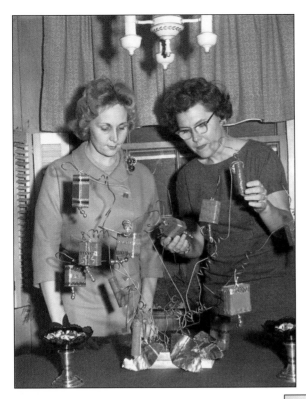

Lucretia Love Tuttle, known to everyone as "Teedie," has been a longtime garden club member. She first belonged to the Cotton Land Club and now is a member of Scotch Gardeners. In 1960, she demonstrates Christmas decorations made out of spice boxes with an unidentified lady. (Courtesy of *The Laurinburg Exchange*.)

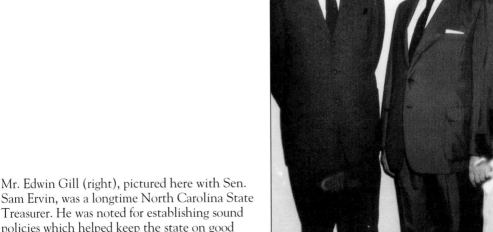

Mr. Edwin Gill (right), pictured here with Sen. Sam Ervin, was a longtime North Carolina State Treasurer. He was noted for establishing sound policies which helped keep the state on good financial footing. (Courtesy of the Gill House.)

34

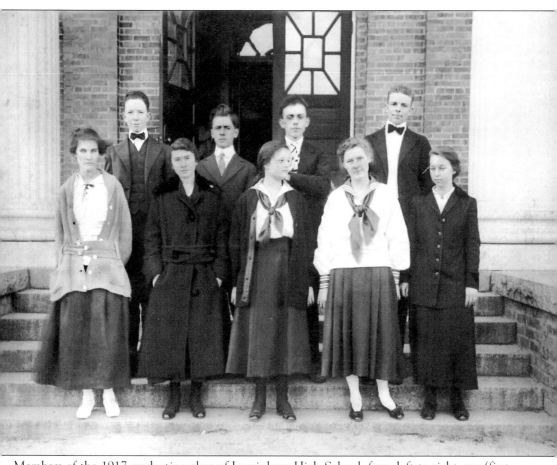

Members of the 1917 graduating class of Laurinburg High School, from left to right, are (first row) Margaret Leach, Sarah Smith, Mary John, Esther "Tom" Stewart, and Thelma Gibson; (back row) Hervey Evans, Colin Hasty, Edwin Gill, and John Wallace. (Courtesy of Scotland County Schools.)

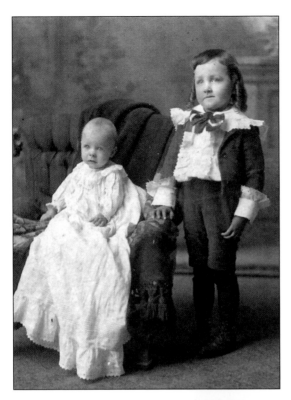

Anna Bella Stewart, born June 3, 1886, and her brother Duncan, born in 1884, pose for portrait in 1890. Duncan died as a child and Anna died in 1975. (Courtesy of Tom Gibson.)

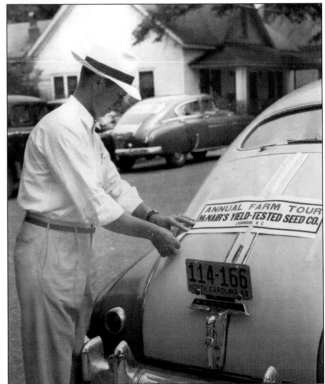

Mr. Fred Harris readies his car in 1949 for the farm tour sponsored by McNair Seed Co. McNair Seed Co. was one of the main industries in Scotland County for many years. (Courtesy of Mutt McCoy.)

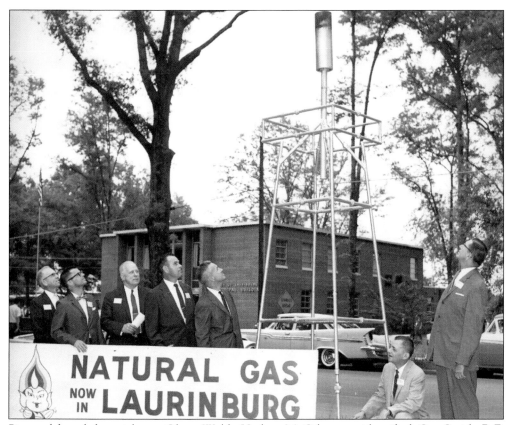

Pictured from left to right are Glenn Webb, Herbert M. Gibson, unidentified, Guy Smith, R.F. McCoy, and Dike Lytch, a group of Scotland County leaders, as they turn on the first natural gas in the county in 1965. (Courtesy of Mutt McCoy.)

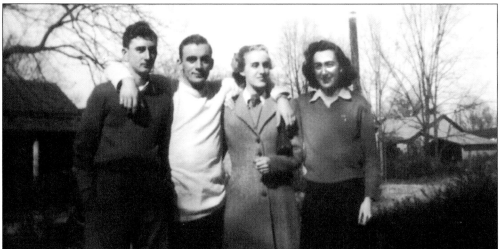

Hugh "Pemo" Stewart, his brother Dan, and sisters Ann and Rosa pose for a snapshot on January 4, 1944. Hugh was active in teaching young people to play sports. The Pemo Stewart baseball league is for students in middle school. Dan, Ann, and Rosa have been active in the county all of their lives. (Courtesy of Ann Nicholson.)

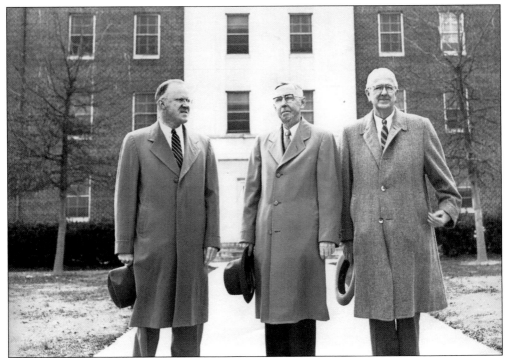

Halbert Jones, president of Waverly Mills; Edwin Morgan, president of Morgan Mills; and Ralph Sanders, vice president and treasurer of Morgan Mills, were all Scotland industrial leaders. (Courtesy of Mutt McCoy.)

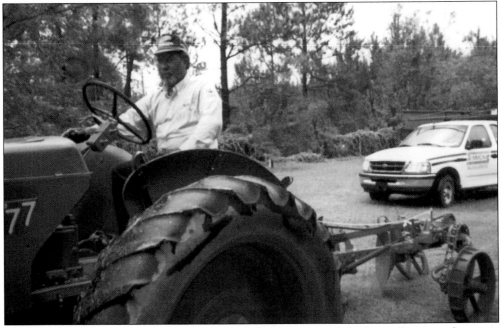

John Frank Stewart, a local businessman and farmer, is noted for his collection of antique tractors. He sponsors an antique tractor show in the spring at the McArthur Farms, south of Laurinburg. (Courtesy of Mutt McCoy.)

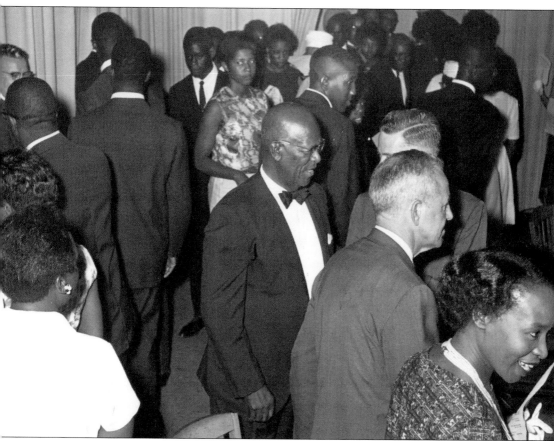

Mr. I. Ellis Johnson was the first principal at the Lincoln Heights School, which was built in the mid-1950s for African-American students in grades one through twelve. He retired in 1965. This picture shows him (in the center) at a reception given for him at the time of his retirement. The school was later named I. Ellis Johnson in his honor. Also identified in the picture are Mr. A.B. Gibson, R.F. McCoy, and Mary Helen Speller. (Courtesy of Mutt McCoy.)

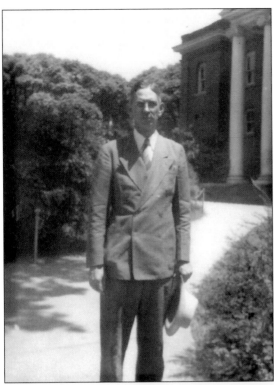

Rev. S.H. Fulton was born in Darlington, South Carolina. He came to Laurinburg Presbyterian Church in September 1930 where he served as pastor until his death in May 1957. He was noted for remarkable sermons and was available to serve whoever called on him. He was active in all segments of the community as well. (Courtesy of Hewett Fulton.)

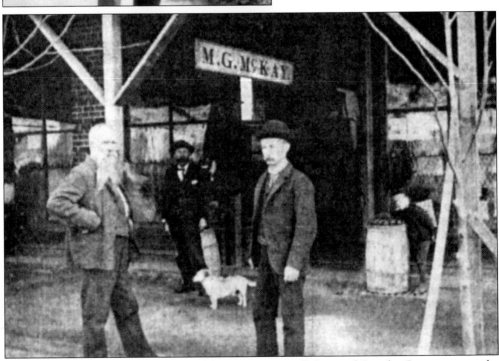

The store at the northeastern corner of the intersection of Main and Cronley Streets was run by M.G. McKay (pronounced McKoy), shown here with the white beard. He was the grandfather of the former Laurinburg mayor, Charles Barrett. (Courtesy of Mutt McCoy.)

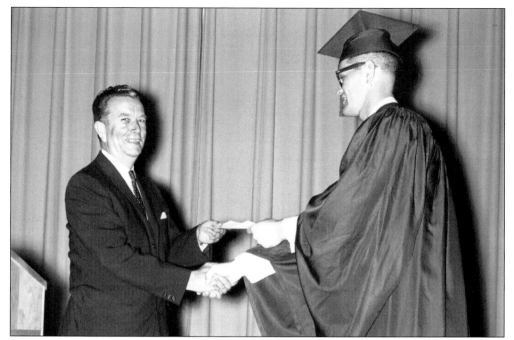

Mr. A.B. Gibson was superintendent of Laurinburg City Schools when it merged with the Scotland County Schools in 1965. Under his leadership the schools had a good reputation for educating all students in the county. He retired in 1969. (Courtesy of R.F. McCoy.)

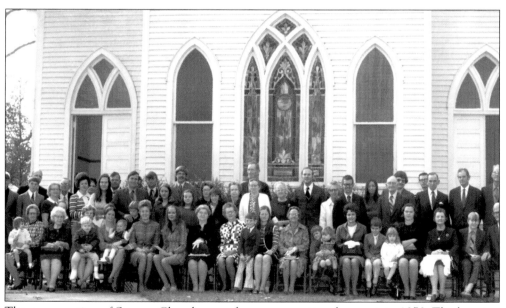

The congregation of Smyrna Church poses for a congregational portrait in 1970. The location of the church, which is far away from the population center, aided in its demise in the late 1980s. (Courtesy of Ginger Gibson.)

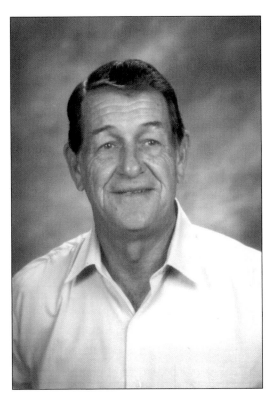

Clyde Parrish was a Laurinburg native. He was a very good high school football player and played in college. He went into coaching, both at the college and high school level. When he retired he was named the "winningest coach in North Carolina." (Courtesy of Scotland County Parks and Recreation.)

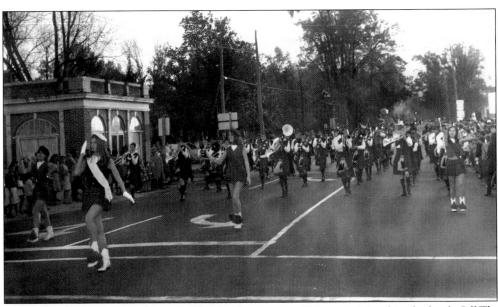

Scotland High School band marched by the former site of Norma's. Listed in the book *Off The Beaten Path*, Norma's was noted for 50¢ dinners and good food. The ravages of time and progress caused the demise of Norma's in the late 1980s. (Courtesy of Renee Snipes.)

Two

PLACES

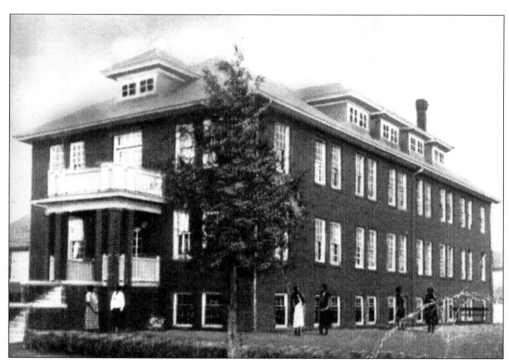

The Laurinburg Institute celebrated its 90th anniversary in September 1994. Notable graduates include jazz great Dizzy Gillespie; National Basketball Association stars Sam Jones, Jimmy Walker, and Charlie Scott; major leaguer Wes Covington; and Prime Minister of Bermuda John Swan. Recently, a charter school was opened on campus for students of Scotland County. The building shown here was one of the early ones. (Courtesy of Beacham McDougald.)

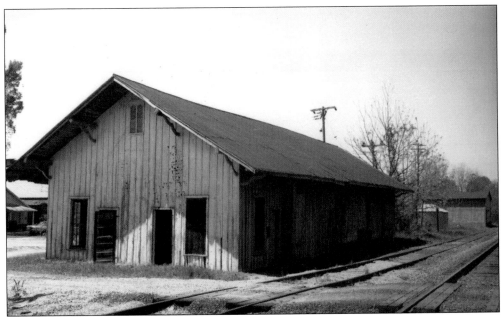

The old Carolina Central Railroad is now part of the CSX Railroad. The depot, which was torn down in 1980, was located in southwest corner of McLaurin Avenue and the CSX RR. Shown is the passenger station prior to 1905. A cotton platform was joined to this, and the area cotton was shipped from it.

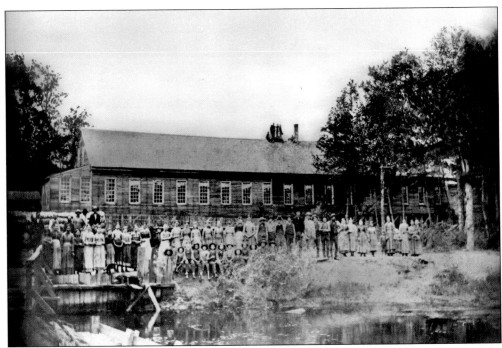

The Morgan Mill at Laurel Hill was an early textile mill in Scotland County. This picture of the mill was made c. 1890. (Courtesy of Jimmy Morgan.)

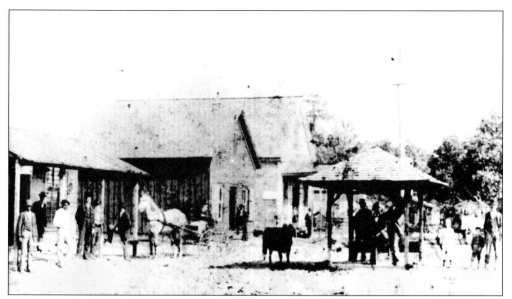

Hasty Community was a bustling community at the time of the formation of Scotland County. (Courtesy of Beacham McDougald.)

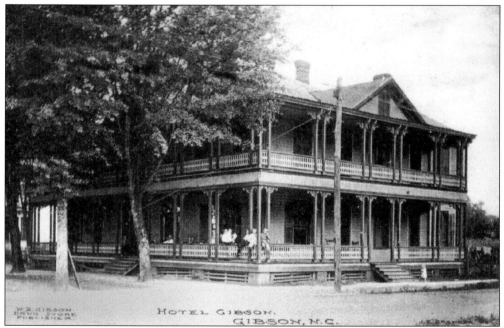

The Gibson Hotel was open for travelers at the beginning of the 20th century. Gibson was an affluent town at that time with the homes of merchants and farmers filling the main street. Time has been hard on Gibson, however, and it has lost some of its shine as well as the hotel. (Courtesy of Beacham McDougald.)

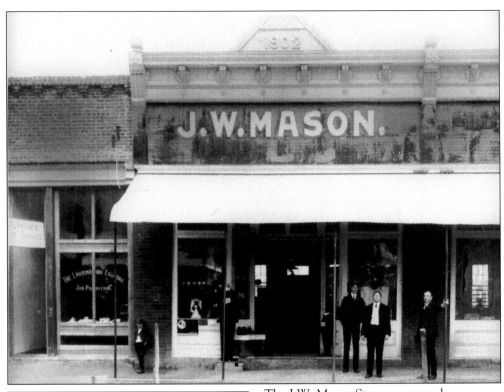

The J.W. Mason Store was an early 20th-century store on Main Street. It was a general mercantile and sold a variety of goods. (Courtesy of Beacham McDougald.)

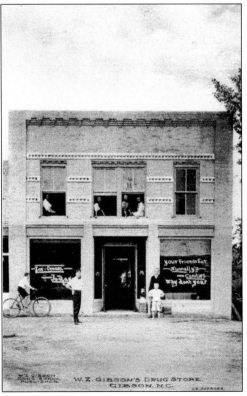

The M.Z. Gibson Drug Store in Gibson is pictured at the turn of the 20th century. Mr. Gibson is a descendant of the town's founder. (Courtesy of Beacham McDougald.)

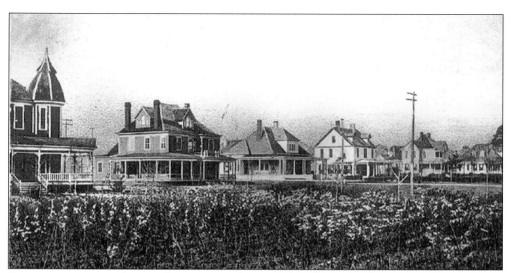

Cotton was grown in the town limits, as seen here on Church Street. This picture was taken from a series of postal cards that were available in the 1910s. (Courtesy of Beacham McDougald.)

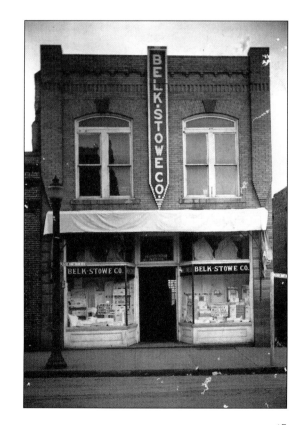

Belk Stowe was the ancestor of our modern Belk store. The Belk stores began in the 1920s and spread throughout the Carolinas. This store was an early one in the chain. (Courtesy of *The Laurinburg Exchange*.)

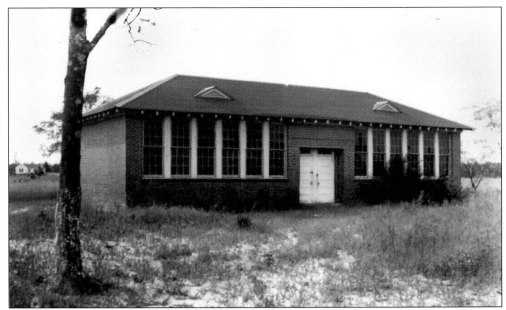

Julius Rosenwald, who made his fortune in Sears Roebuck, gave money to help build at least 12 schools for black children in Scotland County in the 1930s. Most of these schools replaced the one- or two-room schools used before that. By his death in 1932, he had donated $4 million to the construction of 5,000 schools for African Americans in the south. Zion Chapel school, shown here, was one of the schools built with his funds. (Courtesy The Scotland County Schools.)

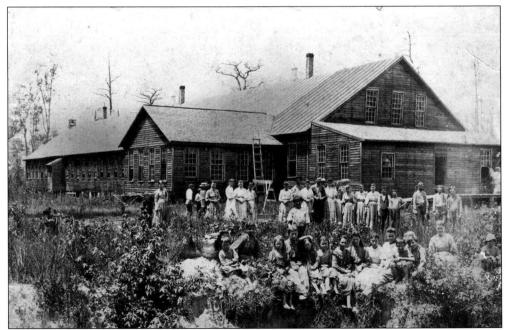

Ida Yarn Mill is pictured here in the 1890s. The employees and their children are pictured in front of the mill. (Courtesy of Jimmy Morgan.)

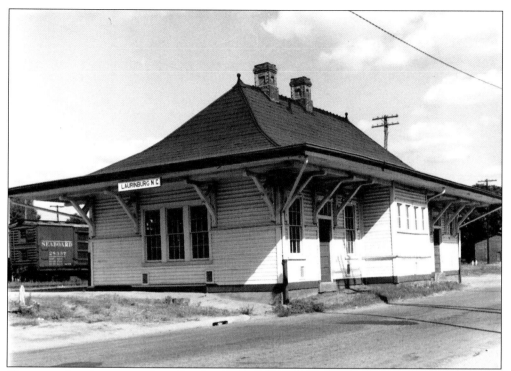

The train played a major role in Scotland County history. Through the early years, the county was served by passenger as well as freight service. This is the picture of the depot in Laurinburg, which has since been razed. (Courtesy of *The Laurinburg Exchange*.)

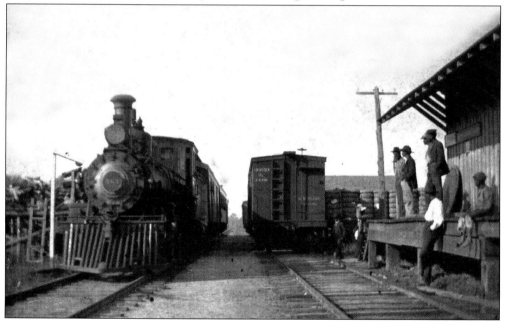

This Atlantic Coast Line Railroad depot was in John's Station, and the name of the town came from this station. The main products shipped from here were melons and cotton. (Courtesy of R.F. McCoy.)

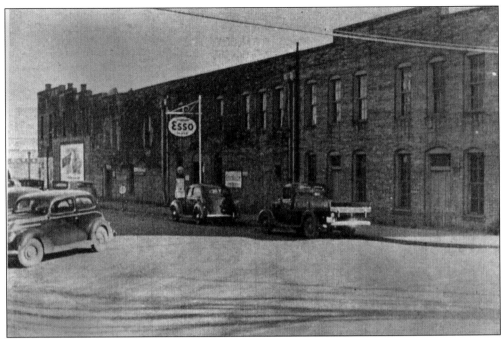

In the 1920s, all Scotland County residents got their gas at this pump, which was located on Roper Street on the sidewalk beside the original McNair's store. This picture was made in the mid-1930s. (Courtesy of R.F. McCoy.)

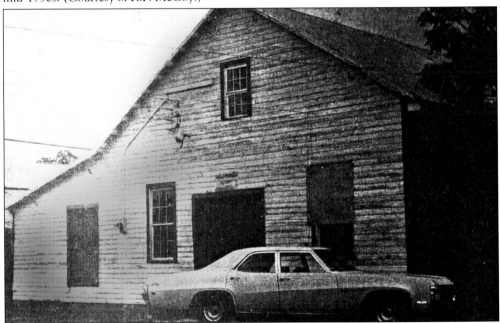

Mr. Zebulon Vance Pate got his start in this building, which operated as the John F. McNair General Store. He joined the business as a clerk at the age of 17. Mr. Pate bought the McNair business on credit in 1900. Edwin Pate, who became the president of Z.V. Pate, Inc. when his father died, guided the business into a massive corporation. The first building still stands in Laurel Hill behind the post office. (Courtesy of R.F. McNair.)

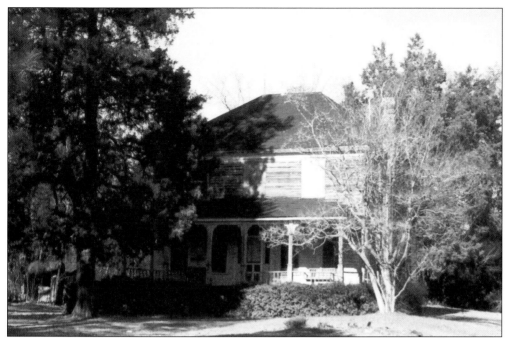

"Ballachulish" is located on Fieldcrest Road in Scotland County. It was built on land purchased by Hugh McLaurin when he emigrated from Scotland in 1791. The present house is the second to be built on the site, replacing one that burned in 1865. (Courtesy of Sara Stewart.)

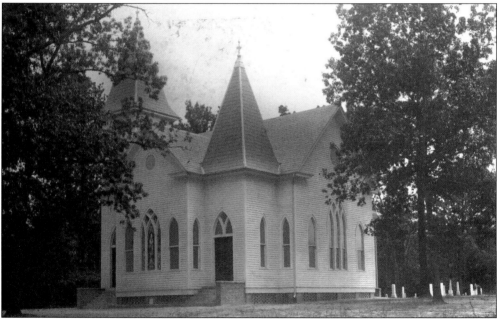

Smyrna Presbyterian Church was located in the southern part of the county. Although it had its roots in a much earlier church, it was formed in 1802. After Smyrna closed in the 1980s its building was moved to the site of Faith Presbyterian Church and is used as the sanctuary. The cemetery remains on the original site and is kept up by a foundation. (Courtesy of *The Laurinburg Exchange*.)

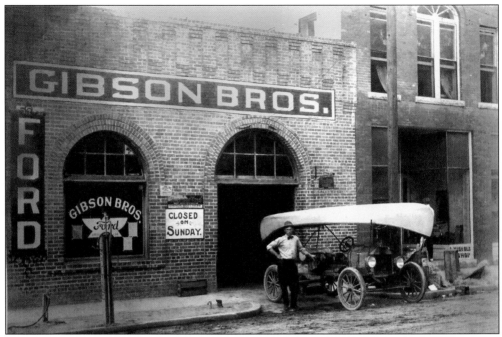

The Gibson Brothers sold Fords until around 1915. Afterwards, Ralph and Jasper purchased the Dodge, Essex, and Hudson franchise. This building was torn down in 1939 and the Gibson Theater was built in 1940. It remained there until the late 1960s. (Courtesy of Reg and Marilyn McVicker.)

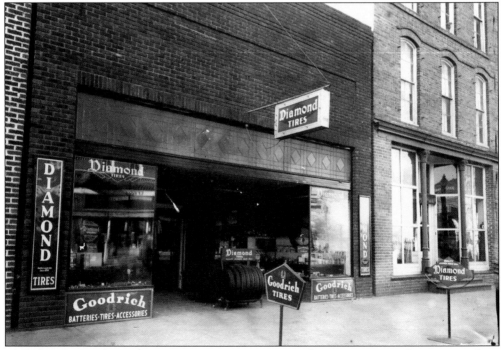

The McLean Supply Company on Main Street in Laurinburg was organized in 1934. It later operated on Roper Street. (Courtesy of Elsworth Stubbs.)

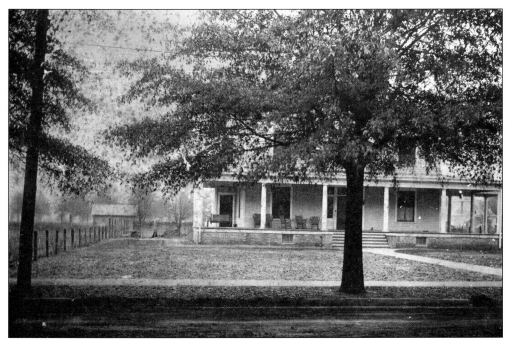

The J.T. Gibson house on East Church Street was built in the late 1800s. (Courtesy of Reg and Marilyn McVicker.)

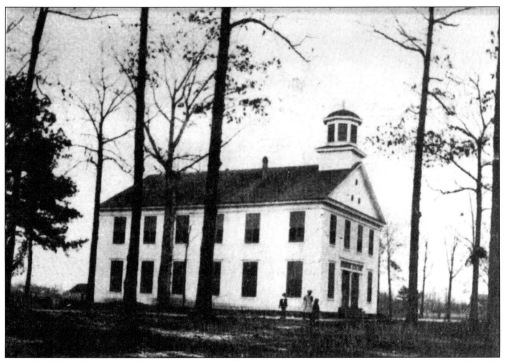

Laurel Hill Presbyterian Church was officially formed in 1797. It has been the "mother church" of many Presbyterian churches in Scotland and surrounding counties. It is still serving the spiritual needs of its members today. (Courtesy of Bo Butler.)

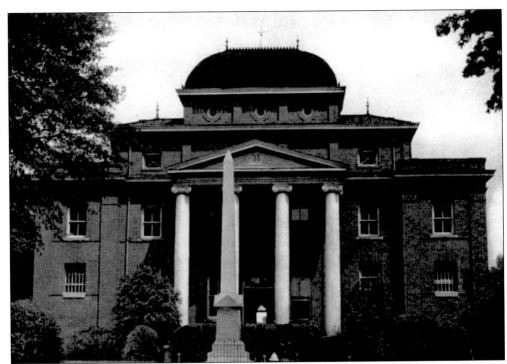

The Scotland County Court House was built in the early 1900s after the county was formed. It served the county on Main Street until the late 1960s when the new courthouse was built. When the old courthouse was razed, opposition came from many Scotland County residents. (Courtesy of Sally Little.)

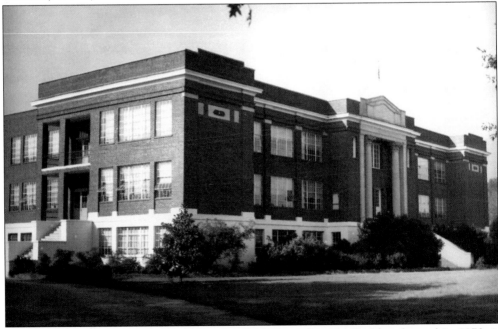

Laurinburg High School stood on East Church Street; when the building burned in 1973, it housed the Laurinburg Junior High School. (Courtesy of *The Laurinburg Exchange*.)

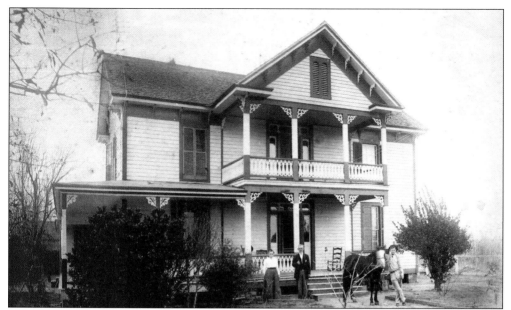

The Captain Wright house was in the northern part of Scotland County. Mrs. Maggie Wright had two sisters, Mary and Sally McMillan, who together had inherited land from their Uncle Joe, and all three had houses built on the land. Mary's and Maggie's houses burned. Sally's house is still standing and is the home of her daughter-in-law. (Courtesy of Dorothy McMillan.)

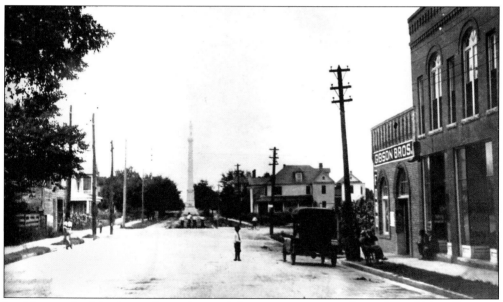

Looking south, this picture shows the confederate monument in the middle of Main Street in Laurinburg. As long as cars were scarce and slow-moving, it remained there. When a signal light became necessary, the monument was moved to the site of the old courthouse; when the old courthouse was torn down, the monument was moved to the new courthouse. (Courtesy of Reg and Marilyn McVicker.)

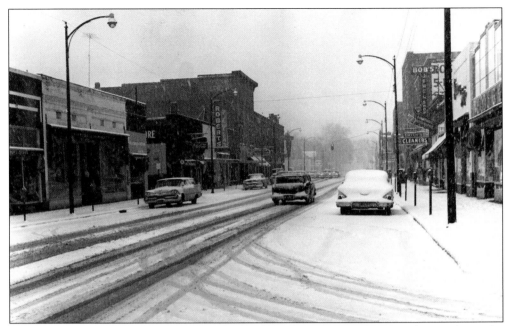

Main Street was covered in snow in this 1960s picture. Snow is unusual enough in the county for the newspaper to get out and take a picture of the excitement. (Courtesy of *The Laurinburg Exchange*.)

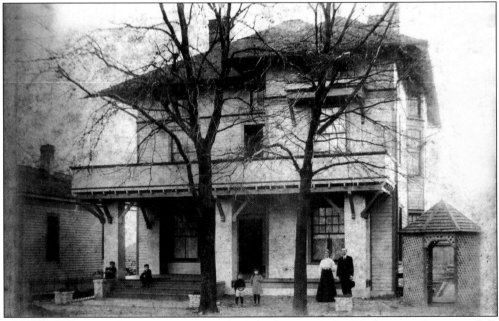

The Gill House was first a one-story structure built in 1884 by Washington Augustus Gill, the first mayor of Laurinburg. The house was remodeled and a second and third story were added. The house was the birthplace of Edwin Gill, private secretary to Gov. O. Max Gardner. Mr. Gill was best known as the state treasurer. The house was given to Historic Properties Commission in 1977 and has been restored with the aid of a grant from the State of North Carolina. (Courtesy of The Gill House.)

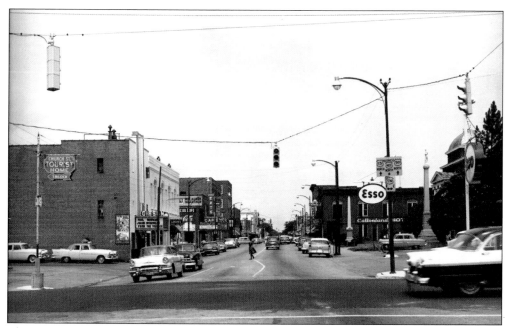

This picture of Main Street was taken in 1959 and shows many businesses that have since closed. Note the Cottonland Hotel to the right. (Courtesy of Renee Snipes.)

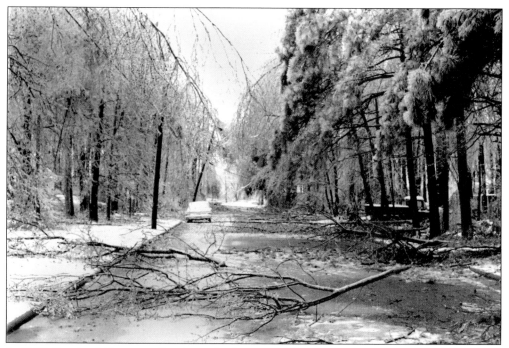

In 1970, Scotland County suffered a major ice storm. The power was out in most of the county for more than a week. In fact, school was out, because without power county schools had no water. (Courtesy of *The Laurinburg Exchange*.)

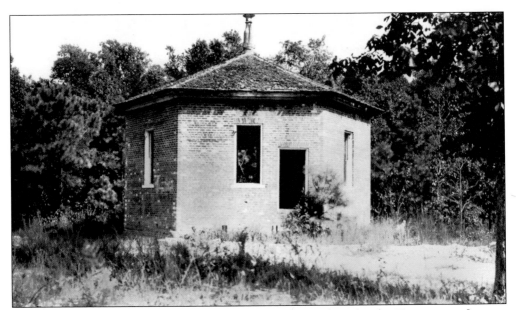

Temperance Hall, near Wagram, was built as a meeting place for the Temperance League, a 19th-century group who fought against the evils of drinking. At the same site is the John Charles McNeil House. John Charles McNeill was a Scotland County native who was once the Poet Laureate of North Carolina. (Courtesy of Margaret Pittman.)

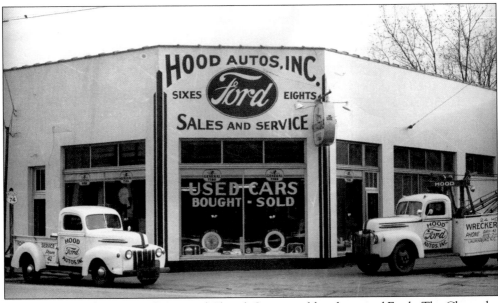

Hood Autos, on the corner of Main and Church Streets, sold and repaired Fords. The Chevrolet dealership was just up the street. The McLaurins and the Hoods were friends and carried on a friendly rivalry . (Courtesy of *The Laurinburg Exchange.*)

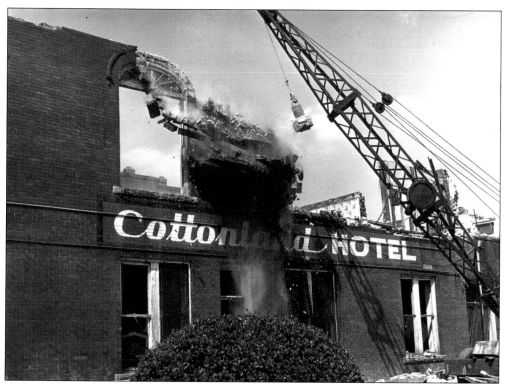

The Cottonland Hotel was first called the Hotel Chewynd. It was on Main Street until it was torn down in the 1960s. (Courtesy of *The Laurinburg Exchange*.)

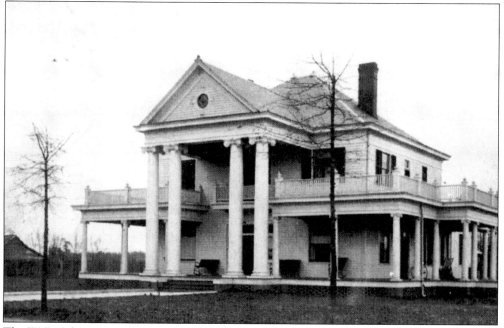

The W.Z. Gibson residence, shown at the turn of the century, remained in the family until the 1980s. It still stands and is in good shape in Gibson. (Courtesy of Beacham McDougald.)

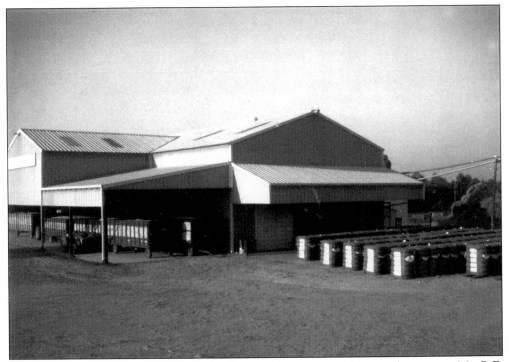

Planter's Gin was opened in 1965 as the first modern automated gin in the county. Mr. R.E. Yongue ran the gin until his death. The site and building is now the school bus garage. (Courtesy of Millie Yongue.)

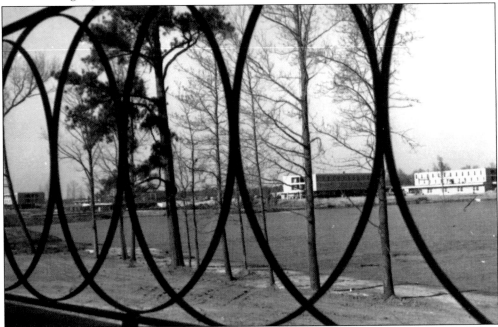

St. Andrews College was formed from the merger of Flora MacDonald College and Presbyterian Junior College in 1961. This view of some of the buildings and the lake is seen through the iron railings on De Tamble Library. (Courtesy of St. Andrews Presbyterian College Archives.)

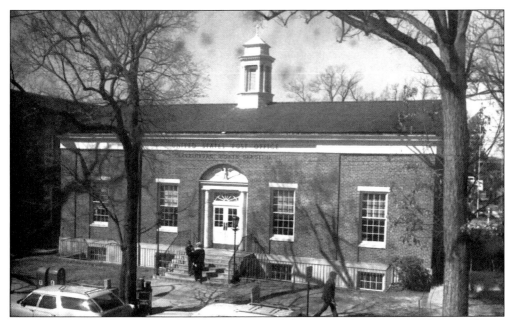

The former post office served the town and part of the county from 1939 until 1978 when a new post office was built nearby. This building is now the Richmond Community College W.R. Purcell Building. (Courtesy of *The Laurinburg Exchange*.)

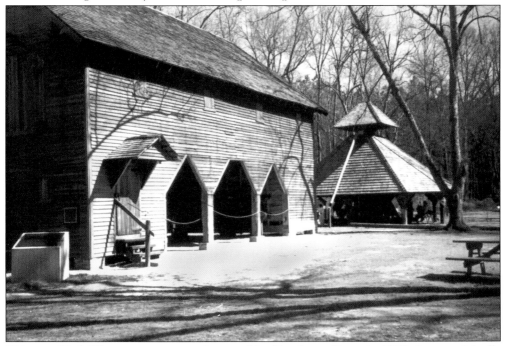

This pre–Civil War cotton gin was destroyed by Hurricane Hugo in 1989. It was originally located in the lower part of South Carolina, but it was given to a group of Scotland County citizens. They rebuilt the gin building to the original specifications. The cotton press was built later in the style of the era. They are located on the grounds of the John Blue House. (Courtesy of Sara Stewart.)

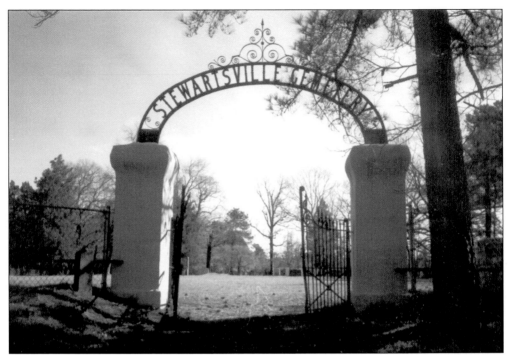

Stewartsville Cemetery is found in the southeastern part of Scotland County. The earliest grave is from the early 1800s, and it is the resting place of many of the early Scottish settlers who came here in 1790. The cemetery has also been used by people with other ethnic backgrounds from the early years until the present. (Courtesy of Sara Stewart.)

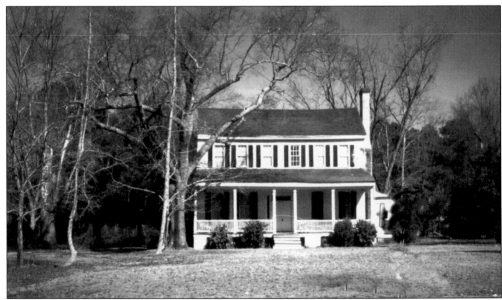

The Stewart Malloy Hawley House stands at the end of the Stewartsville Cemetery Road. It was built by James Stewart, an early settler; it was later sold to the Hawleys who then moved to Connecticut. One of the Hawleys became Connecticut's governor and was the chairman of the nation's centennial celebration. (Courtesy of Sara Stewart.)

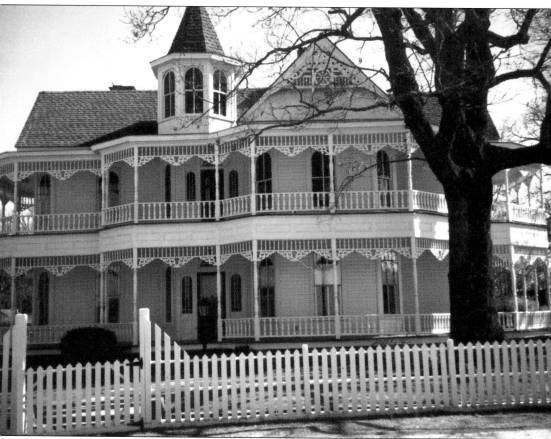

The John Blue family were farmers in the county from early times. Shown is their Victorian-style house, which was built in the 1890s, and houses the Scotland County Parks and Recreation offices. The house was renovated and restored in the 1980s. It is a property of the Historic Properties Commission and is on the National Register of Historic Places. The John Blue Cotton Festival is held on the grounds on the second Saturday and Sunday of October. (Courtesy of The John Blue House.)

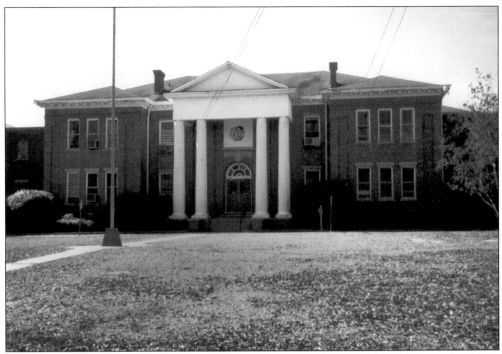

Central School was built in 1909 and was continuously used for classes until December 2000. Before it was closed, it was noted as the oldest public school that was still in use in North Carolina. (Courtesy of Sara Stewart.)

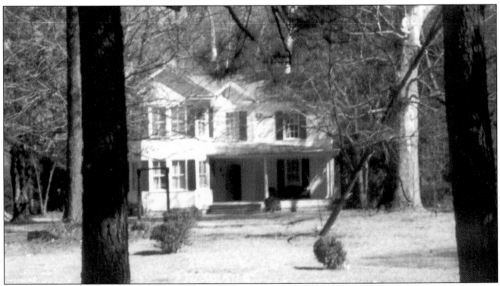

The ancestral home of the Hugh Stewart family, located on King Street, is called "The Farm" by the family because it was out in the country on a farm when it was first built. However, the house is presently very near the center of town. It has been used by several agencies in the county in the past few years. (Courtesy of Ann Nicholson.)

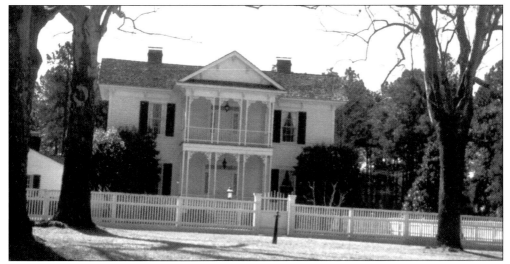

The McRae-McQueen house is located about four miles south of Laurinburg. The original portion of the house was L-shaped and was typical of farmhouses in the early 1800s. The front portion and the kitchen and breakfast room were added between 1820 and 1850. The restoration of the house was begun in 1970 by Mrs. Emma Neal McQueen Morrison who now lives there. (Courtesy of Sara Stewart.)

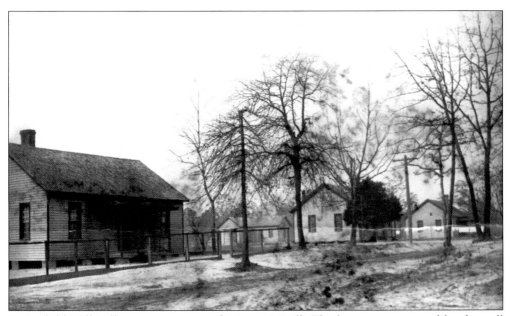

Springfield Mill Village grew up around Morgan's Mill. The houses were owned by the mill until the 1960s. (Courtesy of Jimmy Morgan.)

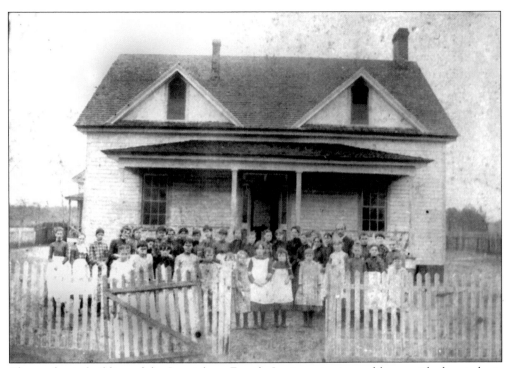

The academic building of the Laurinburg Female Institute is pictured here, with the students and faculty outside. It was located on Church Street and was operating by 1886. (Courtesy of Jimmy Morgan.)

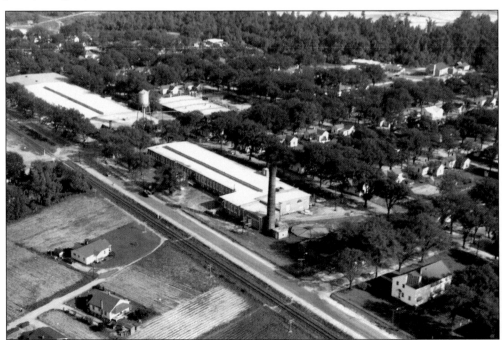

This is an aerial view of a portion of Waverly Mills, Inc. in East Laurinburg. None of the plants there are open now. (Courtesy of Renee Snipes.)

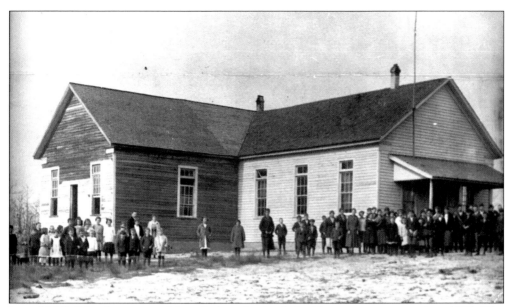

Laurel Hill School is pictured here before the brick building was constructed in 1925. The "new" building was used until 1999 when a new elementary school was built near the town of Laurel Hill. The site of the old school is used by the county parks and recreation department as a community center. (Courtesy of Jimmy Morgan.)

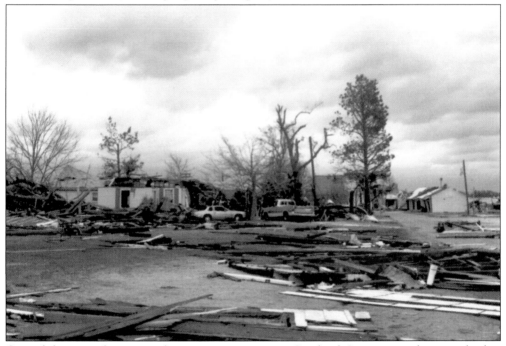

One of the most devastating happenings to occur in Scotland County was the tornado that roared through the southern part of the county on March 28, 1984. One life was lost in the county and extensive damage was done to the area from the South Carolina border, south of Gibson through John's Station and on out of the county to the east. This picture shows some of the damage done in John's Station. (Courtesy of Mac McIntyre.)

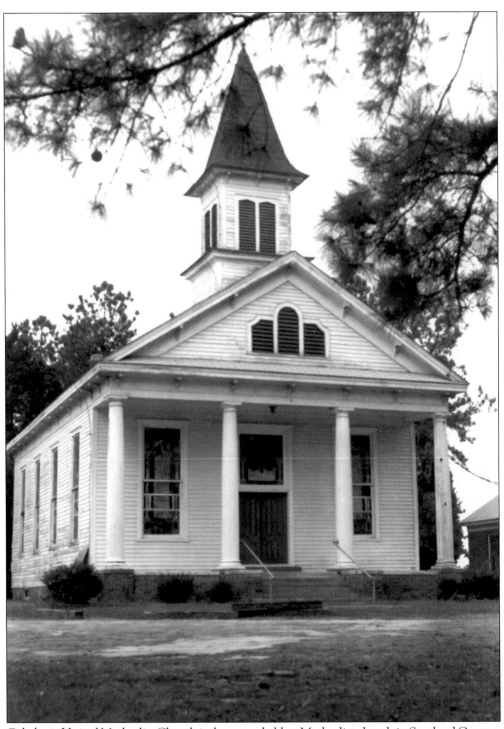

Caledonia United Methodist Church is the second oldest Methodist church in Scotland County. It was organized in 1835 and was called Thompson Methodist Church. Its first minister was Rev. Allen McCorquodale. He renamed the church Caledonia in honor of his native Scotland. (Courtesy of Tom Gibson.)

Three

AT WORK

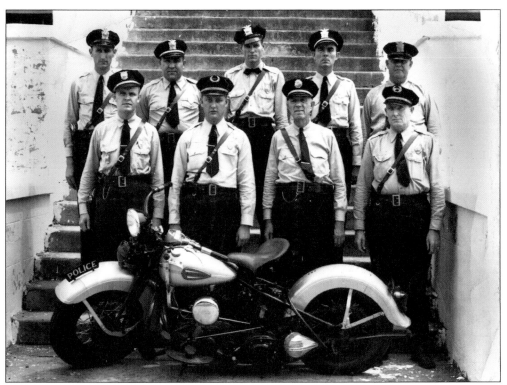

The Laurinburg Police Department poses with their new motorcycle in 1946. They are, from left to right, (front row) R.B. Fowler, Chief West, Sandy Denton, and B.N. McLaurin; (back row) Harry Salmon, J.W. Harvard, ? Dunn, ? Finn, and "Bearhug" Haney. (Courtesy of Mac McLaurin.)

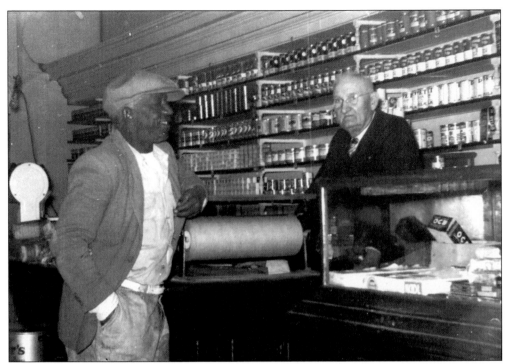

Mr. L.W. Odom ran a general store in Gibson throughout his life. He was the father of Dusty Odom who was a deputy sheriff. (Courtesy of Mary Odom.)

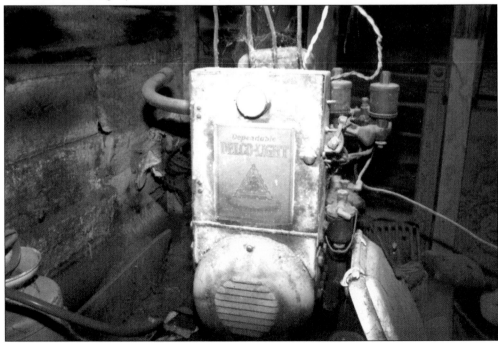

The electricity for the John Blue house was provided with a Delco system after they converted from carbide gas lights. This was early in the 20th century before electricity was available in the county. (Courtesy of Francis Bullard.)

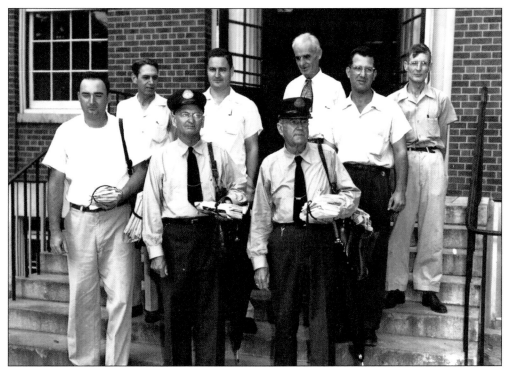

The postal workers at the old Laurinburg post office during the 1950s, from left to right, are (front row) Hugh Stewart, M.L. Walters, and Harry McGee; (middle row) James F. Inman, George Phillips, and Allen McGee; (back row) Postmaster Hugh McArn and Earl McDonald. (Courtesy of Ann Nicholson.)

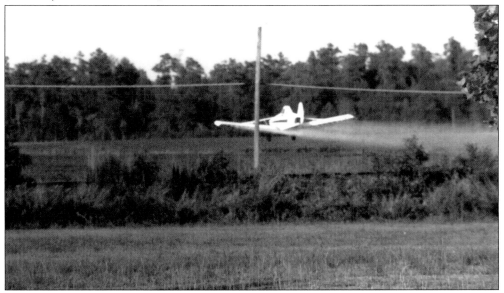

Aerial spraying of crops, especially cotton, began in the 1940s and continued through the 1980s. The airplanes were flown close to the ground as pesticides were sprayed on the crops. The pilots were very talented and would put on such a good show that it wasn't unusual for drivers to line the sides of the road to watch the aerobatics. (Courtesy of Sara Stewart.)

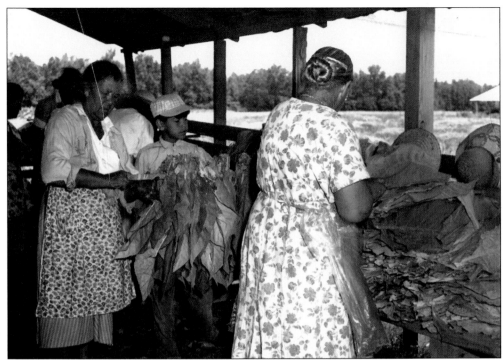

Tobacco was a major crop in Scotland County. Here the ladies and children string the tobacco, getting it ready to "barn." (Courtesy of Sylvia McLean.)

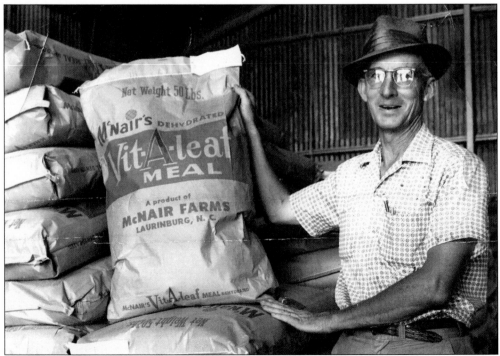

Mr. Hubert McRae is next to bags of dehydrated "Vit-a-leaf" Meal, produced on the McNair Farms in the 1950s. (Courtesy of Sylvia McLean.)

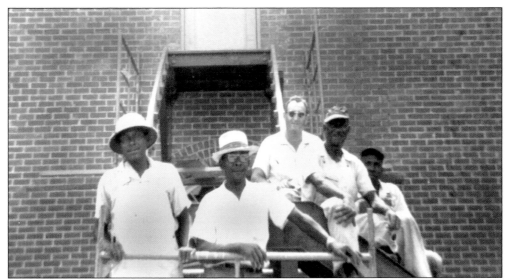

A group of maintenance workers for Scotland County Schools pose at the old Gibson School building. From left to right are Charles Tyson, Preddie Bennett, Frances Bullard, Ed Covington, and James Gilchrist. They were responsible for the upkeep and maintenance of the buildings. (Courtesy of Francis Bullard.)

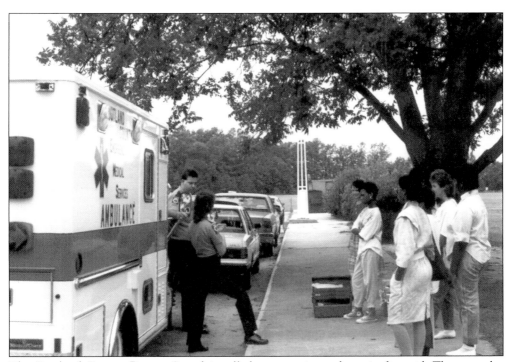

The Scotland County Rescue Squad is called on to train students in first aid. They are also counted on to be present when they are needed. This dedicated group is a blessing to our county. (Courtesy of *The Laurinburg Exchange*.)

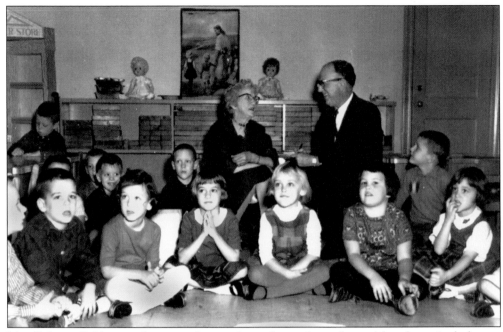

Miss Roberta Coble was a longtime first-grade teacher in Laurinburg. After she retired, she ran the Laurinburg Presbyterian Church Kindergarten. Here she chats with the first president of St. Andrews Presbyterian College who came to speak to the children. (Courtesy of St. Andrews Presbyterian College Archives.)

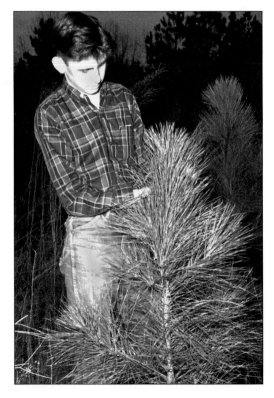

Forestry was part of the agriculture program in the county high schools. Here Ira Ray Newton checks on his young trees in the 1960s. (Courtesy of *The Laurinburg Exchange.*)

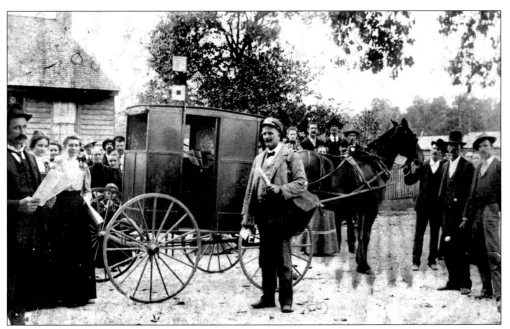

Gerry Wright found this old photograph under the seat of an old car on which he was working. It is a picture of the mail carrier in Gibson in the "horse and buggy" days. (Courtesy of Gerry Wright.)

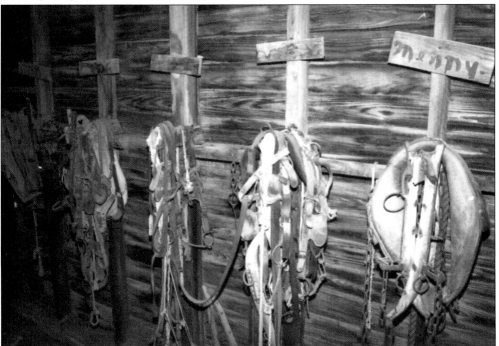

The mules at the Bullard farm were treated well. Mr. Joel Bullard thought it was better for the same harness to be used each time a mule was used. He placed pegs in the wall of the barn and put each mule's name above it, and he always put that mule's harness on the peg. (Courtesy of Francis Bullard.)

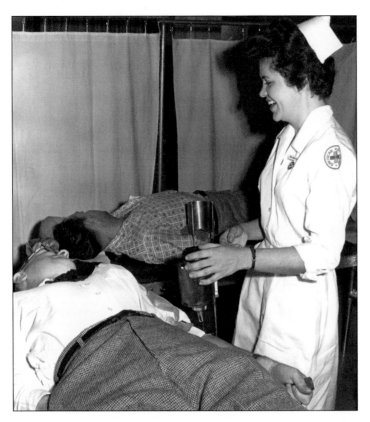

Scotland County citizens give in time of need, as shown here where unidentified donors give blood. The pretty nurse makes it a lot easier on the donors. (Courtesy of *The Laurinburg Exchange*.)

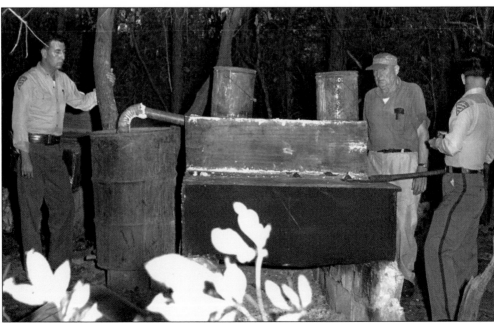

One farmer's "side line" came to an end when this still was raided. The sheriff's department dismantled it. (Courtesy of *The Laurinburg Exchange*.)

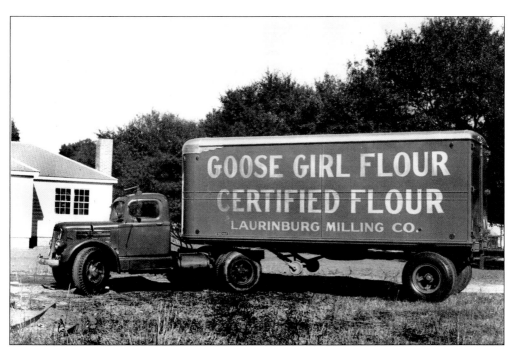

Goose Girl flour was milled in Scotland County for many years. Here is a truck used for delivery in the 1950s. The mill was destroyed by an explosion in the 1970s. (Courtesy of *The Laurinburg Exchange*.)

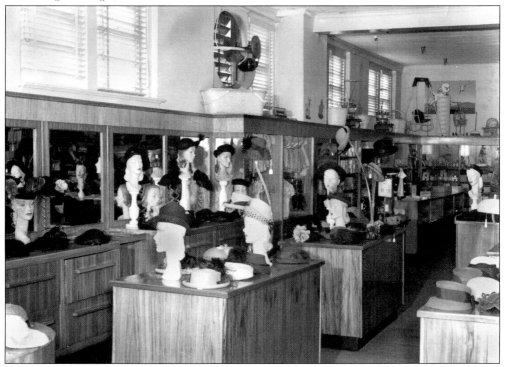

The hat department in the old Belk store was very popular when all the ladies wore hats to church and into town. (Courtesy of *The Laurinburg Exchange*.)

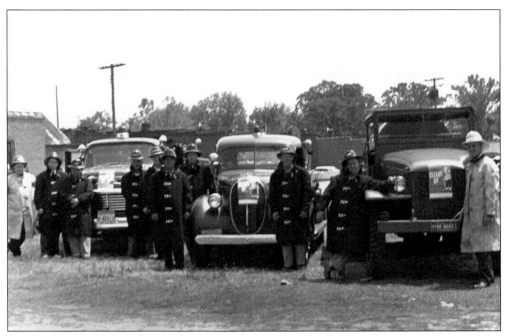

Members of the fire department stand in front of their trucks during a clean-up campaign in the 1950s. (Courtesy of *The Laurinburg Exchange*.)

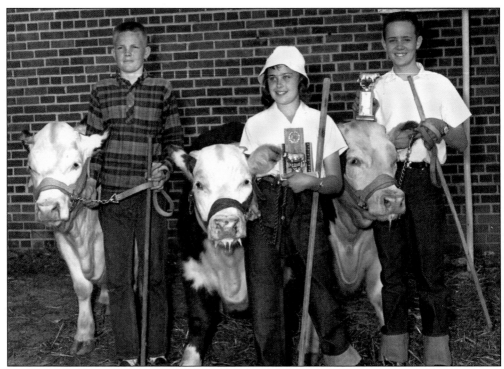

Joe F. McMillan and Susan and Peyton Gentry are shown with their award-winning cattle after a 4-H Beef Cattle Show in the 1960s. (Courtesy of *The Laurinburg Exchange*.)

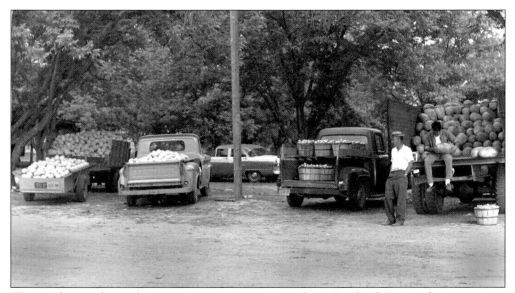

Watermelons and cantaloupes were major crops in southern Scotland County for many years. Here the growers brought them to the farmers market to sell in the 1960s. (Courtesy of *The Laurinburg Exchange*.)

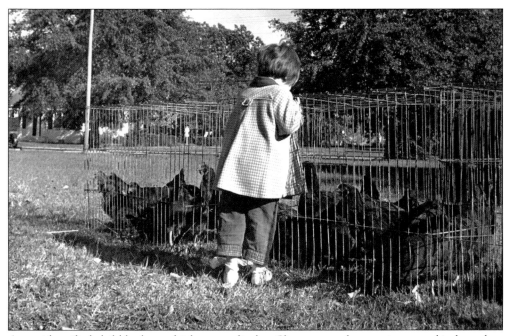

An unidentified child looks at chickens on display. She seems to be very interested in how they are doing. (Courtesy of *The Laurinburg Exchange*.)

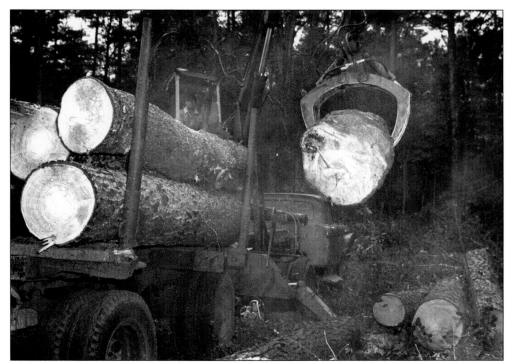

Logging is still a major industry in Scotland County. Many farmers plant pine trees, which they will harvest in the future. Most also replant so that their descendants can reap the benefits as well. (Courtesy of *The Laurinburg Exchange*.)

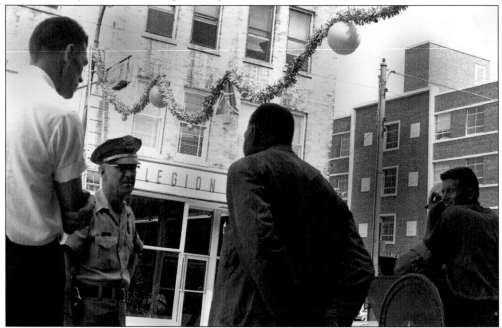

Roy Harris, a city policeman, talks with unidentified citizens during the Christmas season. Each year the town has a Christmas parade to usher in the season, and the streets are decorated before the parade. (Courtesy of *The Laurinburg Exchange*.)

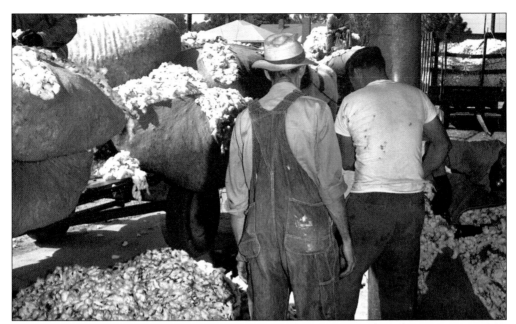

John K. Bennett and others admire the first bale of cotton ginned in the county in 1960. (Courtesy of *The Laurinburg Exchange*.)

Cotton, which is still the major farm crop in the county, was brought to the gins in Scotland County by mule and wagon as well as by truck through the 1960s. Today, the cotton is compacted in the field and is brought to the gin on large trailers. (Courtesy *The Laurinburg Exchange*.)

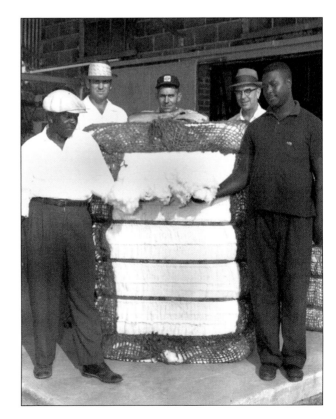

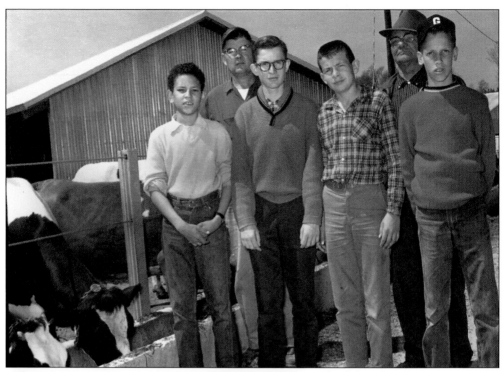

The Silver Cup Dairy was on the Aberdeen Road north of Laurinburg. It was in production through the 1970s. Here several unidentified 4-H members visit the dairy to learn about milk production. (Courtesy of *The Laurinburg Exchange.*)

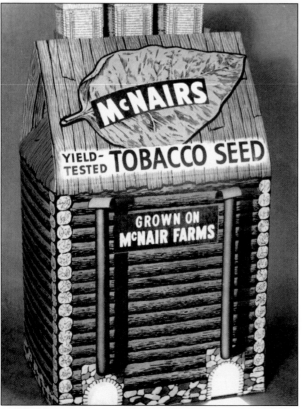

McNair Seed Company was noted for tobacco seed, but they also developed a wonderful sweet corn that you can no longer find. They were the forerunners in innovative packaging as shown here. (Courtesy of R.F. McCoy.)

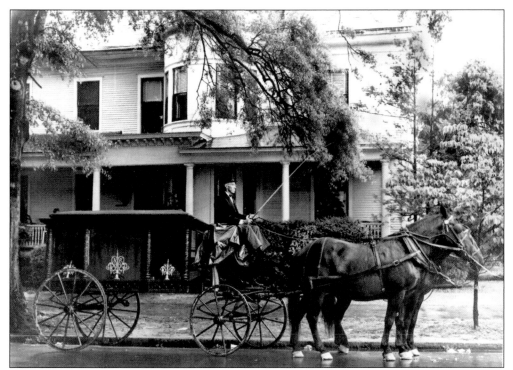

McDougald's Funeral Home was established in the 1880s and has been in the same family ever since. This photo shows a horse-drawn hearse that was in service before the advent of the automobile. (Courtesy of Lulla Thompson.)

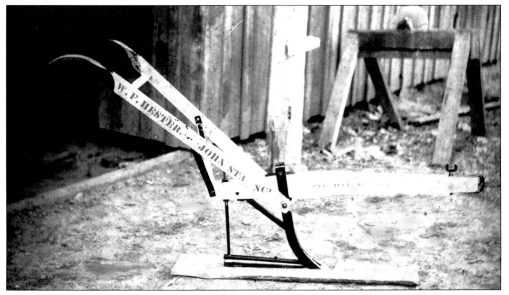

Mr. W.F. Hester, who resided in the John's area of Scotland County, invented this plow. It was patented July 10, 1905. (Courtesy of R.F. McCoy.)

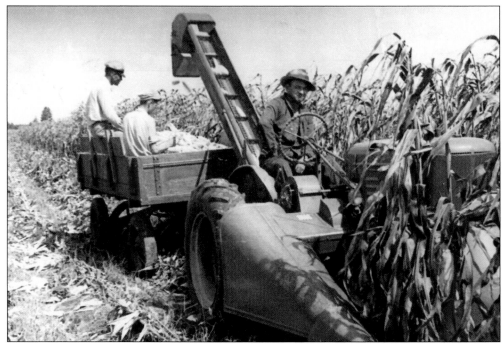

Charles Myers is seen here driving a corn harvester in 1949. The tassels were removed from the stalks that produced the seed corn. The tassels were left on the stalks that produced pollen so that the correct cross-pollination would take place. (Courtesy of R.F. McCoy.)

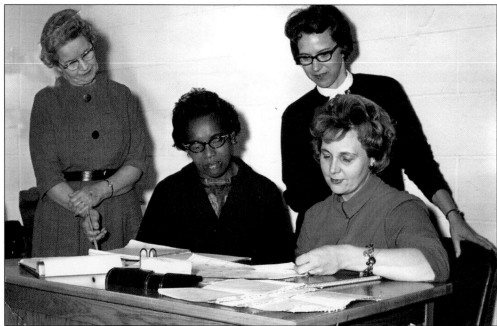

Claire McCallum, Mary Rocher, Vertie Harding, and Teedie Tuttle worked for the Department of Social Services. Their job was to investigate the needs of the county residents and provide information about where they could get help. This photo was taken in the 1960s. (Courtesy of Teedie Tuttle.)

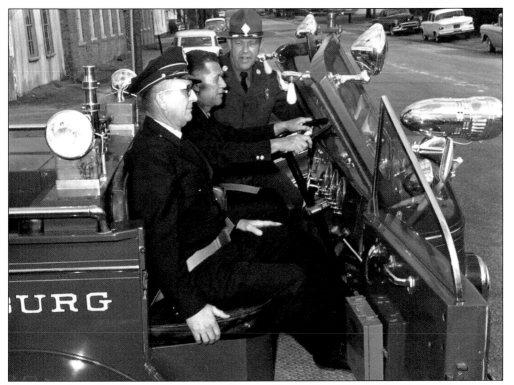

The Laurinburg Fire Department shows off a new fire engine in the early 1960s. (Courtesy of *The Laurinburg Exchange.*)

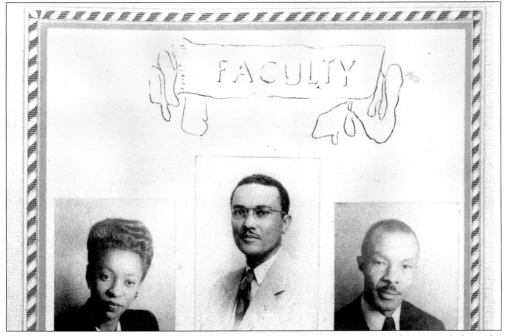

This picture of the Shaw Gin in Wagram in western Scotland County shows how people brought their cotton to the gin in the early 1900s. (Courtesy of Beacham McDougald.)

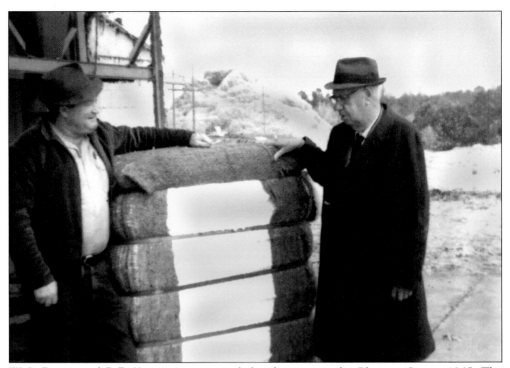

W.C. Bracey and R.E. Yongue examine a bale of cotton at the Planters Gin in 1965. The ginning of cotton was all mechanized and automated, so very few employees were needed. (Courtesy of Millie Yongue.)

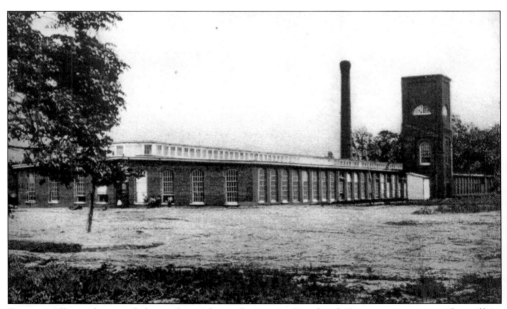

Dixon Mill, evidence of the industrial revolution in Scotland County, was a textile mill in Laurinburg. (Courtesy of Beacham McDougald.)

86

Four

AT PLAY

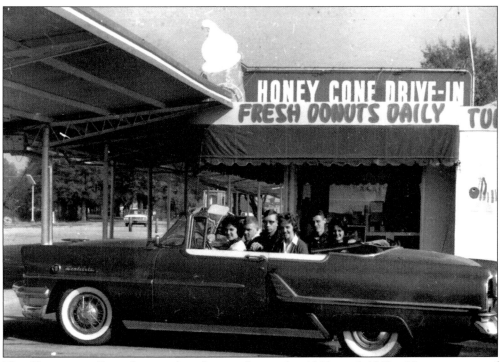

The Honeycone Drive-In was the place to be in the 1950s and 1960s. Here, a group of unidentified teenagers swing into the Honeycone, where people would show off new cars, see old friends, and meet new ones. (Courtesy of *The Laurinburg Exchange*.)

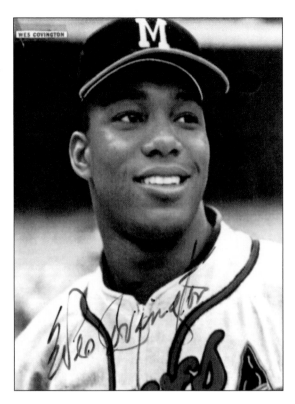

Wes Covington was a native of Laurel Hill in Scotland County. He was a graduate of The Laurinburg Institute, and he played Major League Baseball with the Milwaukee Braves. (Courtesy of Scotland County Parks and Recreation.)

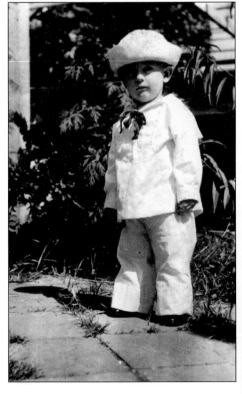

"I don't know who he is but isn't he cute in his spiffy sailor suit?" Several old pictures were given to the John Blue House with no identification, and this one of a little boy was one of them. (Courtesy of The John Blue House.)

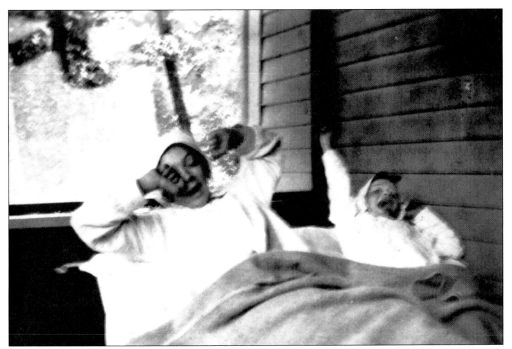

The sleeping porch is a Southern institution. Before air conditioning, the porch would catch any cool breezes that might be stirring on hot summer nights. These girls seem to have enjoyed a good night's sleep. (Courtesy of The John Blue House.)

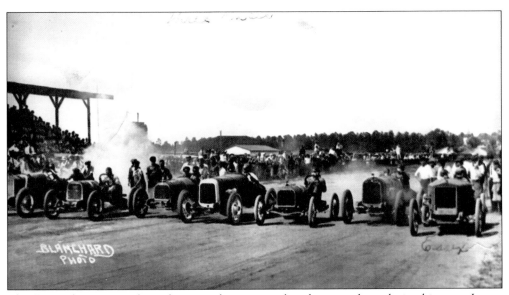

The Essex, first car on the right, won the time trial and sat on the pole in this race. It was owned by the Gibson Brothers of Laurinburg and was driven by Bill Liles. (Courtesy of Reg and Marilyn McVicker.)

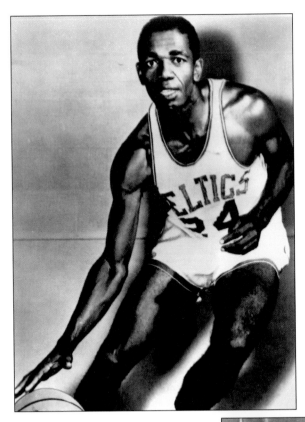

Sam Jones was a Scotland County Native and a graduate of the Laurinburg Institute. He played basketball for the Boston Celtics and was just one of the many who played professional ball after graduating from this esteemed school. (Courtesy of Scotland County Parks and Recreation.)

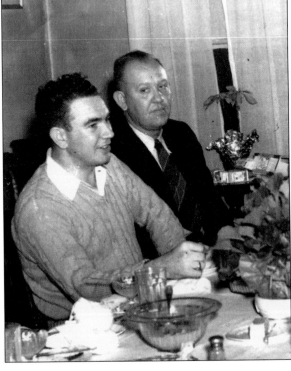

Professional baseball player "Puddin Head" Jones is shown as a guest of the police department in 1946. Jones was a native of Laurel Hill and played with the Philadelphia Phillies. Later he toured the Carolinas and went by the title of "Clown Prince of Baseball." (Courtesy of Mac McLaurin.)

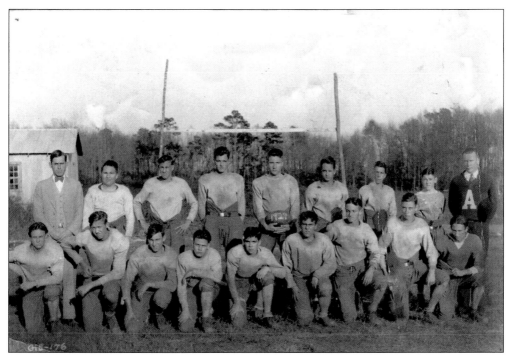

This was the football team from Gibson High School in 1929. In the early days, the small schools played in a 5-man football league, which allowed the smaller schools to have football teams. This continued in North Carolina into the 1950s. (Courtesy of Mary Odom.)

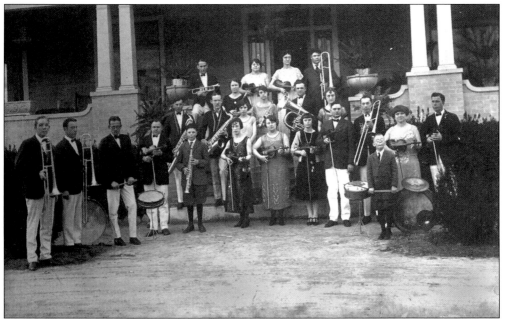

We know Gibson as a very small town, but in earlier days it was considered to be quite busy, with several doctors, a drug store, and an orchestra, which is shown here. In the days before television, many people learned to play musical instruments to provide entertainment for the town. (Courtesy of Mary Odom.)

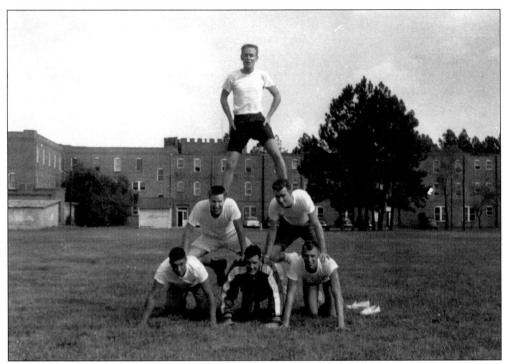

John Stewart (top) and Doug Yongue (second row, right) goof off while students at Edward's Military Institute in 1956. Mr. Yongue knew how to get ahead—he is now a state representative. (Courtesy of Millie Yongue.)

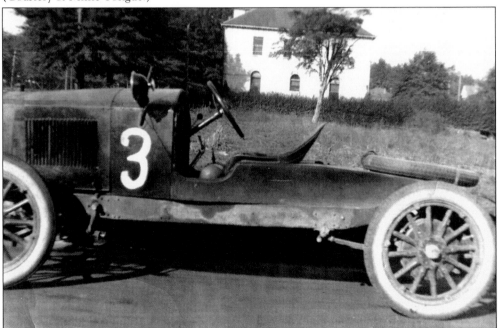

The late Ralph and Jasper Gibson converted an Essex family touring car into a racer in 1919. The racer made a brilliant record on dirt tracks in the southeast from 1919 until 1921. In the 1950s, Tom Gibson restored a replica of this Essex. (Courtesy of Reg and Marilyn McVicker.)

These unidentified young people model their homemade Easter bonnets for the newspaper camera in the 1960s. (Courtesy of *The Laurinburg Exchange*.)

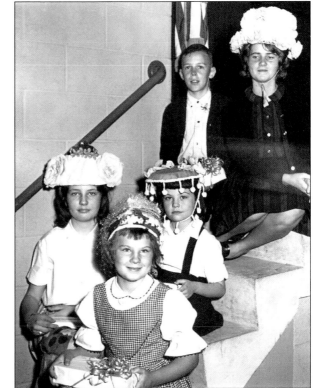

The Scotland High School band has been invited to play in several well-known parades including the Macy's Thanksgiving Day Parade; they have played at Disney World at least once. They are shown here playing in the Azalea Festival Parade in Wilmington, North Carolina. (Courtesy of Sara Stewart.)

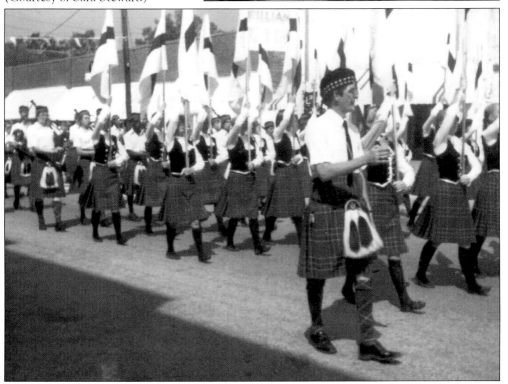

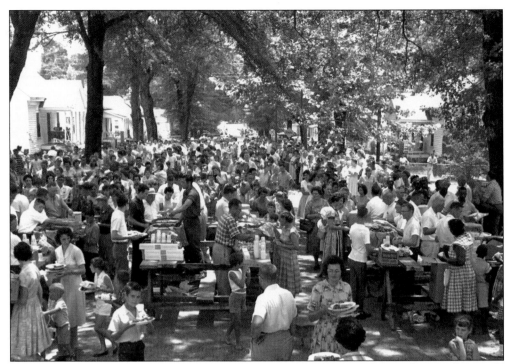

The Fourth of July picnic was held each year in East Laurinburg for the employees of Waverly Mills. This photograph was taken in the 1960s. (Courtesy of *The Laurinburg Exchange*.)

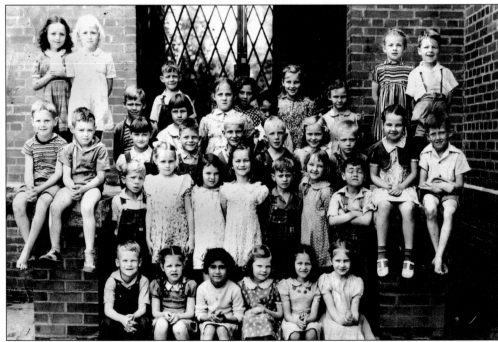

Mrs. Mary Phillips's first grade class of 1941 poses on the steps of Central School. There were two first grade teachers at Central School at this time. Miss Roberta Coble taught the other class. (Courtesy of Teedie Tuttle.)

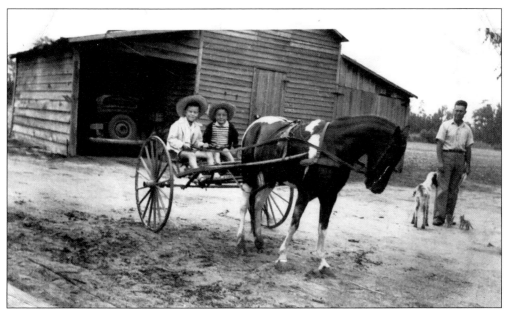

Woodrow Thompson looks on as his sons Dick and John Ed ride in the pony cart. This picture was taken on their farm near Hasty in the 1930s. The horse was named Tony. (Courtesy of Tom Gibson.)

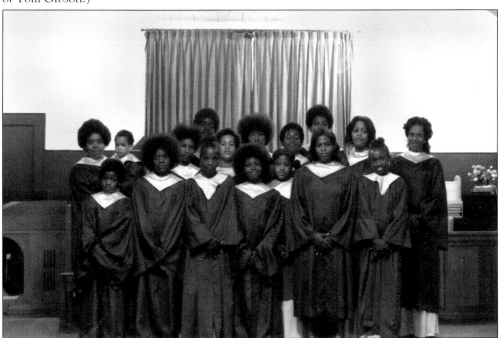

The junior choir at Spring Branch Missionary Baptist Church provided a lot of fun for the young people and added joy to the church service. Shown here, from left to right, are (front row) Darren Gilchrist, Leisa Caple, Vaunzell Wells, Quenzella Caple, Beverly Massey, Brenda Gilchrist, Lorrain Wells, and Maud Wells; (back row) Annie Neil Massey, Daisy Ann Tyson, Reginal Massey, John Willie (Beaver) Gilchrist, Cathy Gilchrist, Oscar Leroy (Butch) Wells, Patrick Cole, and Winona Massey. (Courtesy of Maude Wells.)

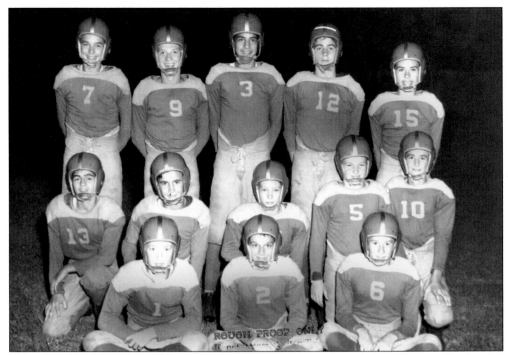

A group of men—Earl Bradley, N.W. Quick, Pemo Stewart, and Doc Haigwood—decided to organize a midget football league in 1950. Interest in the youth was high and they were able to form four teams from the county youngsters. Pictured here is the championship team of that year.

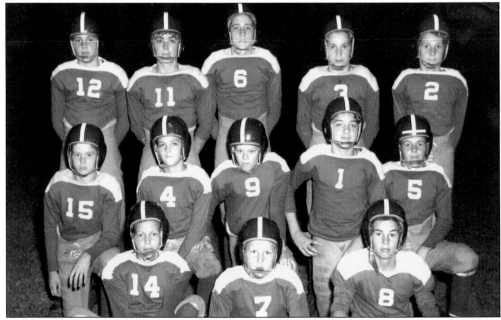

Coaches for this league were Earl Bradly, Hugh "Pemo" Stewart, and Thomas "Doc" Haigwood. The team members learned the fundamentals of the game and many were players in high school.

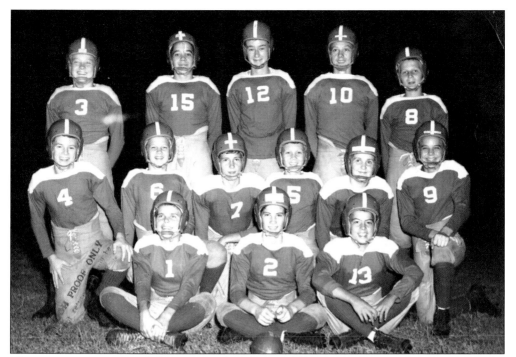

The community sponsored the teams so that they could have matching uniforms and all of the equipment. Earl Bradley is the only coach that is still living. (Courtesy of Earl Bradley.)

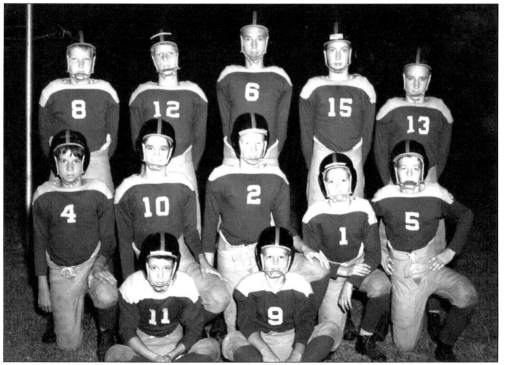

These boys are scattered all over the country now. They have never had a reunion but some talk has been heard about trying to get together since these photos turned up.

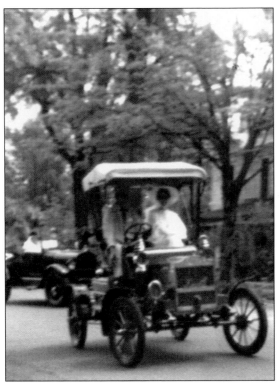

The Scotland County celebration of the bicentennial of the United States included a parade. Here are two of the antique cars that are owned by Scotland County citizens. (Courtesy of Sara Stewart.)

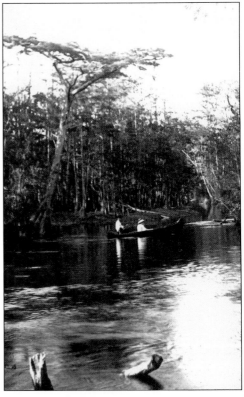

Riverton, near Wagram, was a community on the Lumber River. Over the years it grew to be a thriving area. The river here was the swimming hole for much of the county and was once a county park. It is now part of the national scenic river system and is part of a new state park that is being developed. (Courtesy of R.F. McCoy.)

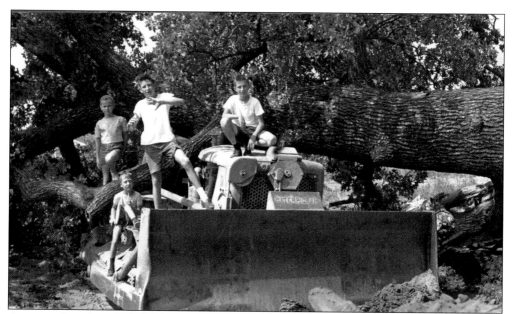

A group of unidentified children play on a bulldozer that was hit by a falling tree. They aren't going anywhere but can you imagine what adventures they are pretending to have. (Courtesy of *The Laurinburg Exchange*.)

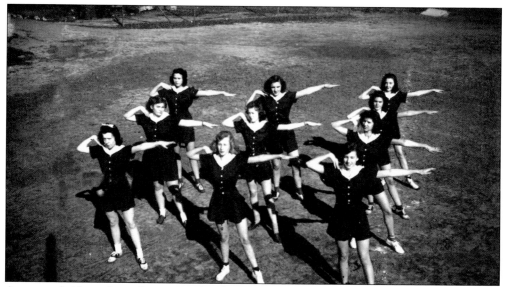

A group of girls performed a routine for physical education class at Laurinburg High School in 1943. P.E. is still required for at least one year at the high school level. (Courtesy of Scotland County Schools.)

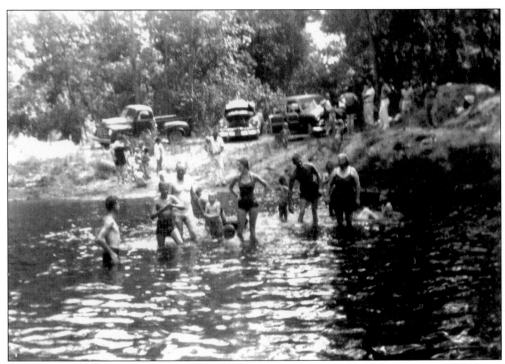

Juniper Creek, a favorite swimming place for many years, is north of Laurinburg on Highway 15-501. It has a reputation for having the coldest water around. (Courtesy of Sylvia McLean.)

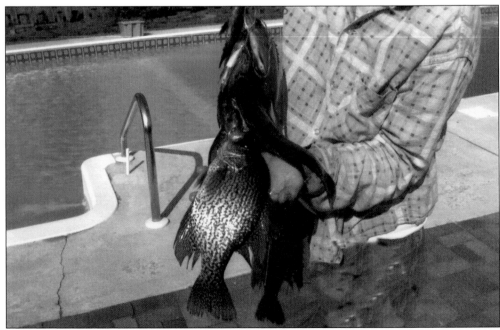

Fishing is a popular pastime in the county. An afternoon on a peaceful pond could also provide a good meal. Here a boy poses with his long string of fish. (Courtesy of Sara Stewart.)

Five

CELEBRATIONS

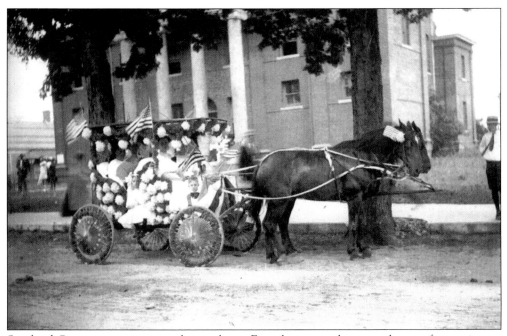

Scotland County citizens enjoy their politics. Even long ago, they were known for putting on a big show for their favorite candidate. Here is a group riding in a decorated cart for a political rally. (Courtesy of Beacham McDougald.)

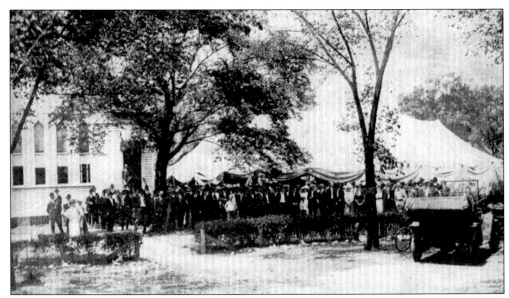

There was a Great Methodist Revival in May 1912. This is from an old postcard, which was sold locally. (Courtesy of Beacham McDougald.)

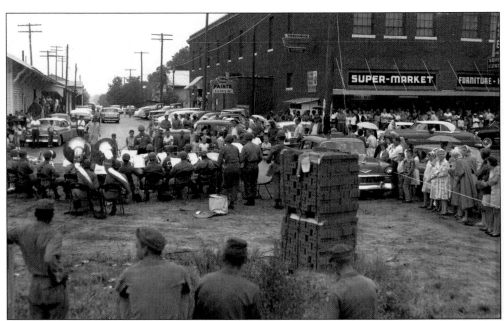

A mystery surrounds this picture. It was made in Laurel Hill around 1955 and a large crowd is present with the army band playing. Several longtime residents were asked if they could identify what was going on, but no one could. (Courtesy of *The Laurinburg Exchange*.)

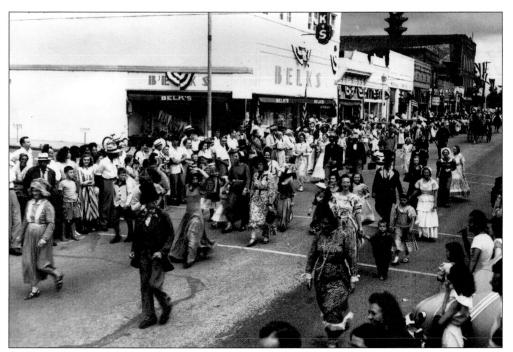

Scotland County citizens celebrate the bicentennial of the United States with a fancy dress parade. (Courtesy of *The Laurinburg Exchange*.)

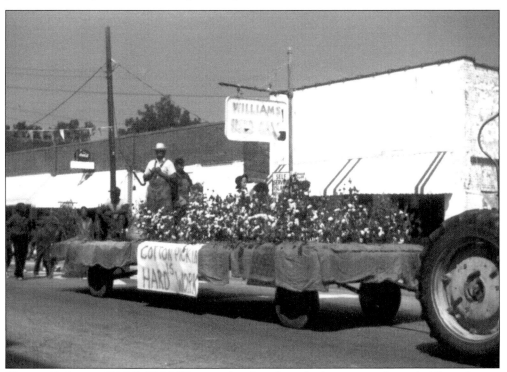

"Cotton Picking is HARD WORK" states this float from the bicentennial parade. The riders on the float are unidentified. (Courtesy of Sara Stewart.)

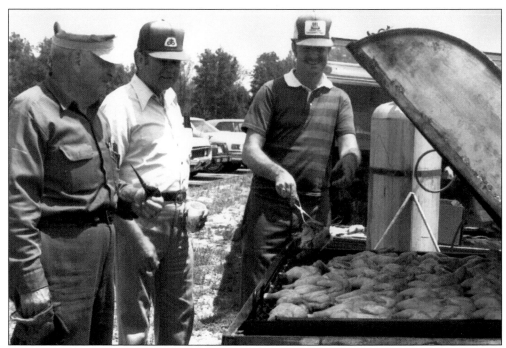

Francis Bullard, Khan Perkins, and Colin McArthur cook barbecued chicken for a Homemakers' Club fund-raiser in the 1980s. They all are known for good cooking. (Courtesy of Francis Bullard.)

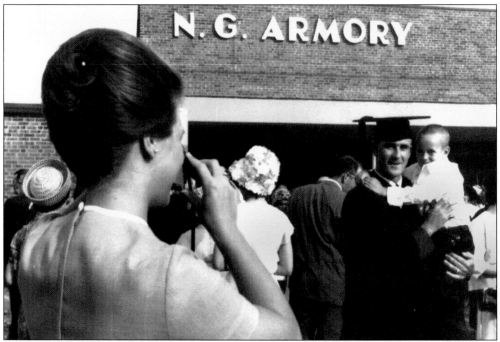

St. Andrews College opened in 1961 and the first graduation was held at the National Guard Armory. A graduate poses with a family member after graduation. (Courtesy of St. Andrews Presbyterian College Archives.)

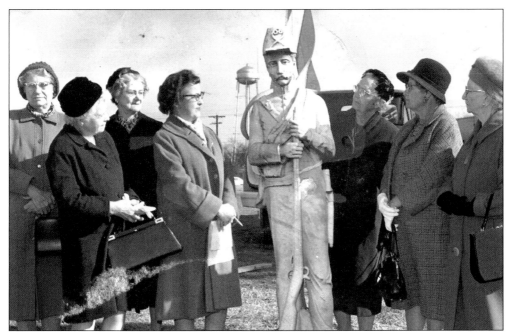

After cars became so numerous that a traffic light was necessary at the corner of Main and Church Streets in Laurinburg, the Confederate monument was removed to the site of the Scotland County Court House on Main Street. When the new court house was built in 1964, it was moved there. Standing with the statue in this photograph, from left to right, are Mrs. Carl Parker, Mrs. Anna Meta Purcell, Miss Lucy McCormick, Mrs. Mozell Parker, Miss Emily Patterson, Mrs. W.L. Thrower, and Mrs. P.L. West Jr. (Courtesy of Elsworth Stubbs.)

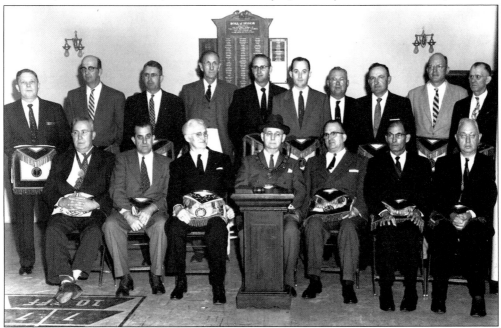

The installation of officers of the Laurinburg Masonic Lodge is seen here in 1949. (Courtesy of Millie Yongue.)

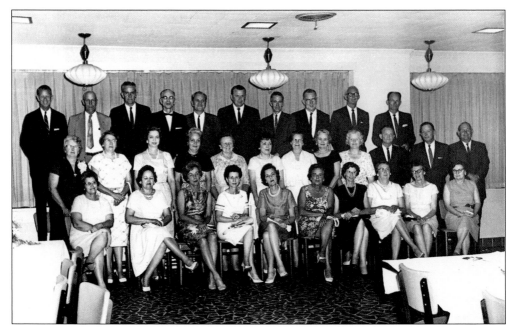

The Laurinburg High School class of 1931 attends a class reunion in 1964. Shown, from left to right, are (front row) Lola Thompson, Julia Bracey, Willie Smith, Lila Brigman, Elizabeth James, Ollie Leak, Annette Hester, Mildred Willis, Myrtle Snead, and Evvie Hudson; (middle row) Mary Margaret McCormick, Gladys Jones, Loreen Hicks, Carrie Mae Callahan, Flora Thrower, Rachel Norton, Mary Norton, Elizabeth Blue, Mable Livingston, Reynolds Sutherland, Jim Sutherland, and Oscar B, McCormick; (back row) Robert Everett, Pate Currie Earl Hearn, Hubert Jones, Butris Anthony, John Monroe Jones, Charles Barrett, Glen McCall, Tom Gibson, and Hunter Murray. (Courtesy of Reg and Marilyn McVicker.)

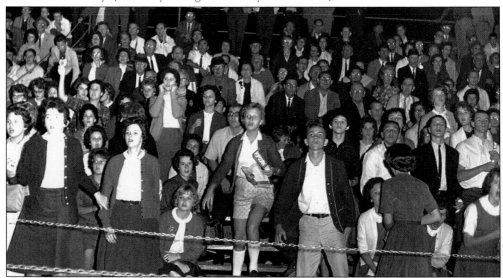

The crowd at the Laurinburg High School football game was very excited about something. We could guess that the game was with Rockingham, since they have always been our biggest rival. We hope it was one of the rare times when Laurinburg beat them. (Courtesy of *The Laurinburg Exchange*.)

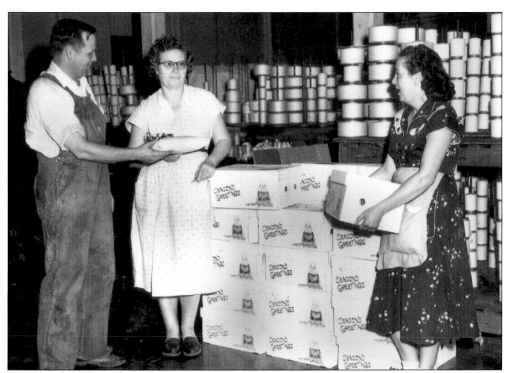

Waverly Mills employees Ralph Wagner, Nell Polston, and Beulah Butler fix Christmas boxes for the employees in the 1950s. (Courtesy of Joyce Braswell.)

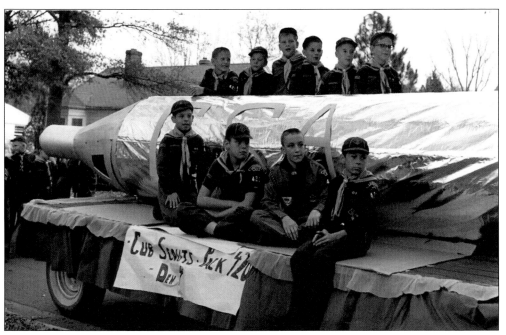

Unidentified cub scouts of pack 420 ride on a rocket float in 1950s parade in Laurinburg. (Courtesy of *The Laurinburg Exchange*.)

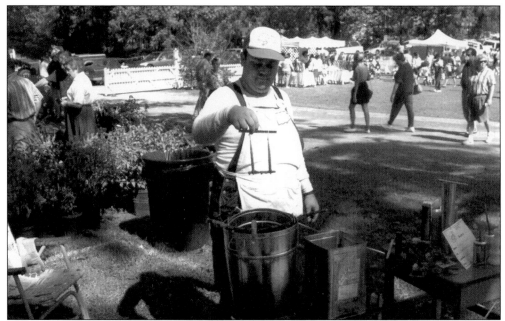

Alan Stewart demonstrates the way to make candles by dipping them at the John Blue Festival. This festival is held the second weekend of October each year. (Courtesy of Sara Stewart.)

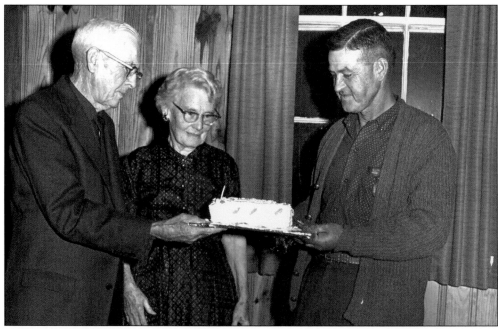

The Scotland Farmers Club presented Mr. and Mrs. Joe Arch McMillan with a birthday/wedding cake on November 16th, 1961. It was Mr. McMillan's birthday and the couple's 51st wedding anniversary. The cake is presented by H.C. Newton. (Courtesy of *The Laurinburg Exchange*.)

Six

INGATHERINGS

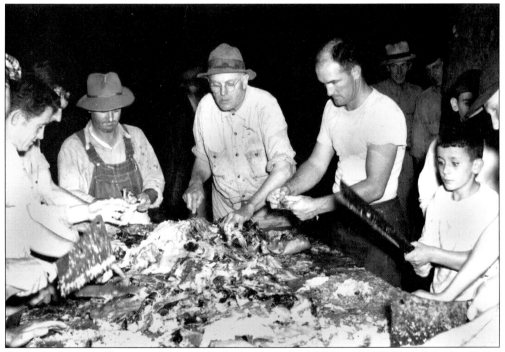

A group of men and boys cut the meat for barbecue at the Old Laurel Hill Church in the 1940s. Those identified are Fred Currie (fourth from left), Eli Murray (fifth from left), John McLean (second from right), and Archie Mclean (far right). (Courtesy of Sylvia McLean.)

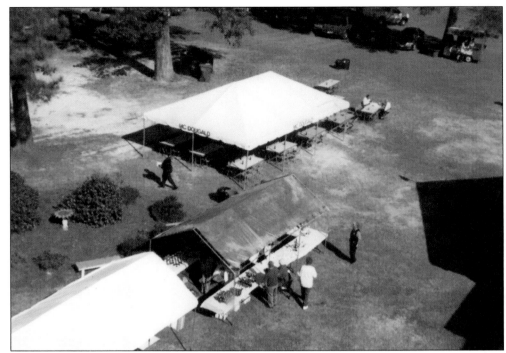

On Thursdays from the middle of October until the middle of November, many churches in Scotland and surrounding counties celebrate the phenomenon called Ingathering. These pictures were made at Laurel Presbyterian Church, but the process would be similar in all the older churches in the area. (Pictures in the rest of this chapter are courtesy of Old Laurel Hill Presbyterian Church.)

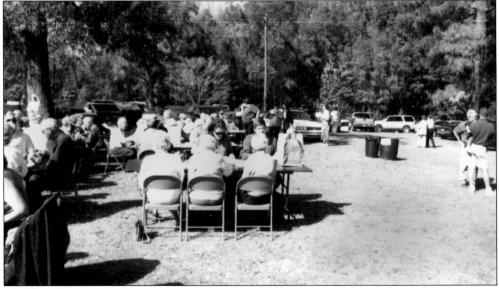

Ingatherings were started as a way to finance the mission of the churches in the early 1930s —deep in the Great Depression when money was short. The farmers brought produce, bales of cotton, and provided pigs for barbecue. The women made cakes, crafts, and quilts as their contributions.

110

After cooking on gas cookers all day, the pigs are now done. The men unload them on clean tables and chop the meat until the choppers are satisfied.

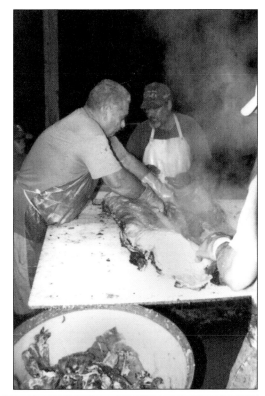

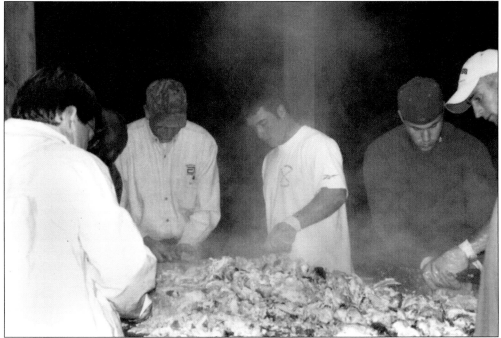

The chopped meat is refrigerated overnight; early in the morning the "cooking down" begins. There, delicious barbecue sauce is added. Each church has its own sauce recipe and is famous for their own flavor.

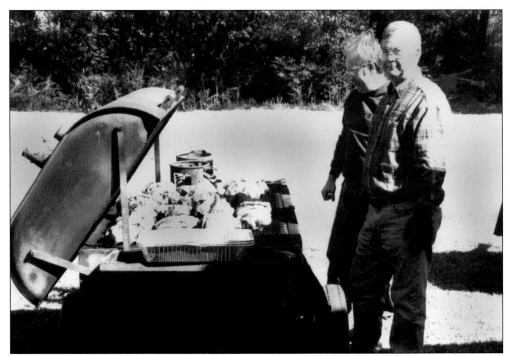

Some churches serve barbecued chicken as well. They are cooked on grills and another type of barbecue sauce is added. They are the second most popular item on the day's menu.

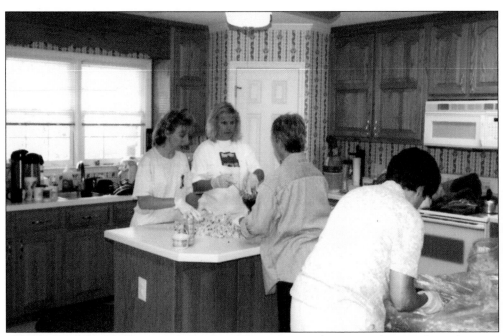

Chicken salad is served at some churches. The women volunteer to buy, cook, and cut up chickens, which they bring to a central place. On the morning of an ingathering, all the ingredients are combined and bagged. They are kept cold in coolers until time to be served. As with recipes for sauces, each church has a special chicken salad recipe.

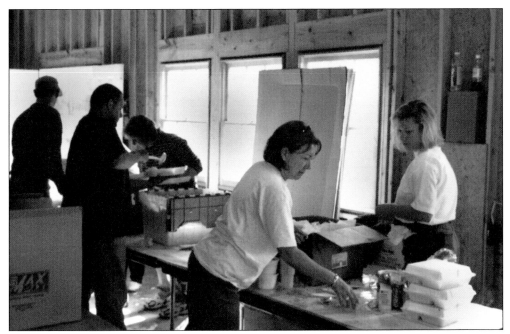

When all the church members are gathered, the day is started with a devotion. Then the serving begins. At Laurel Hill, only lunch is served. Carry-out trays are delivered all over the county and sometimes beyond. Some other churches serve only supper, and some serve both.

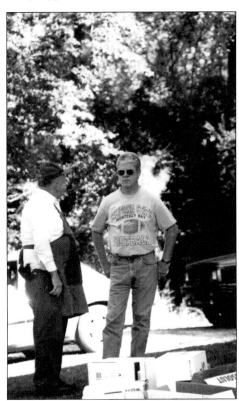

Fred Fox, a local radio personality, helps church member Harry Smith collect boxes for the carry-out plates.

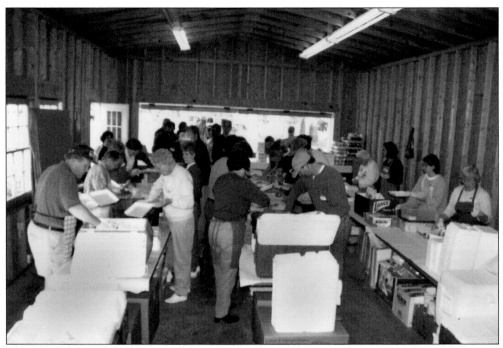

These churches are generally small. Many friends and family members join in to serve the many plates sold to our visitors.

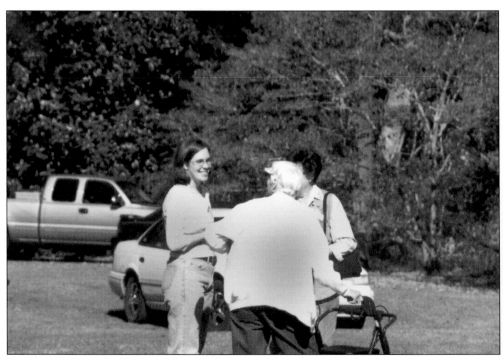

Ingatherings are fund-raisers, but perhaps more importantly they provide a chance to get together with friends and family. Here Jennifer Hansen greets Olis Stubbs and Dottie McMillan.

A multitude of people gather to get their plates. This aerial picture was taken from the church steeple.

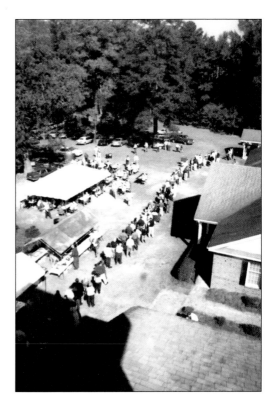

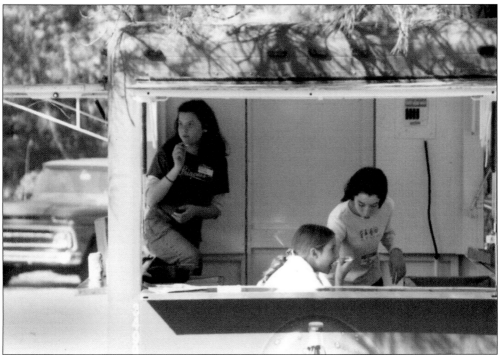

Young and old work together for the good of all. Here Callie Newton, Kate McRae, and Caitlin Monroe serve soft drinks during the day.

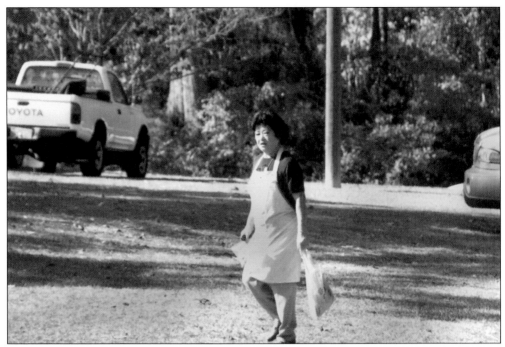

Keiko Fore keeps all the workers in aprons and name tags. She also bakes wonderful yeast breads for sale. Cakes, crafts, canned goods, plants, produce, and snacks are also sold by the church members.

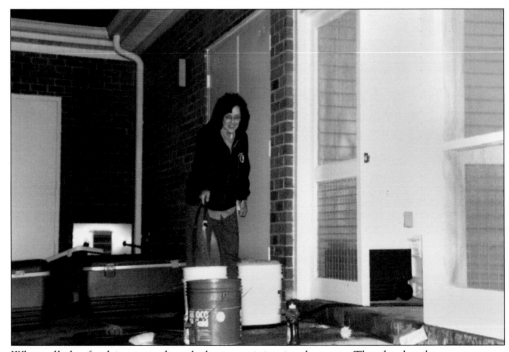

When all the food is gone, the whole group joins in clean up. The day has been a success. Everybody is bone-tired but happy. The tradition forms bonds between the members.

Seven

Old-timey Hog Killings

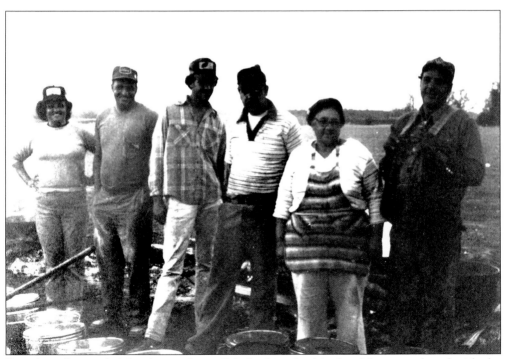

Friends and extended family members all helped in the big day. Meat was shared with the helpers. Pictured here, from left to right, are Savannah Harris, Herbert Clark, Ben James Clark, Carl Dean Clark, Norma Lowery, and Martin Clark Jr. (Courtesy of Mary Lois Clark.)

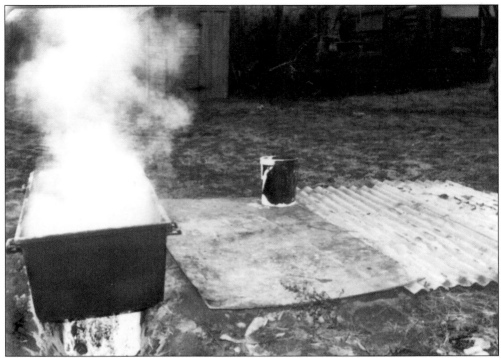

In days gone by most residents of the county kept hogs for meat. Mary Lois Clark shared these pictures of a hog-killing day at her parents' home so we could see how it used to be done. First, the water needs to be heated to a temperature of 140 to 150 degrees to scald the hogs. This helps in removing the hair off the hogs.

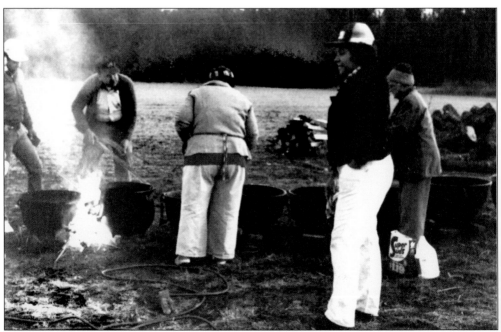

Boiling water is also needed in order to clean the pots and other equipment.

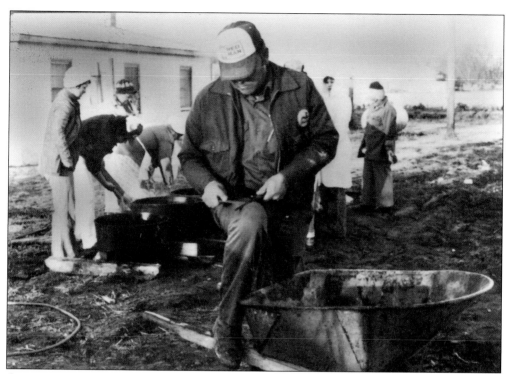

Gurney Bullard sharpens his knives, because the knives need to cut cleanly.

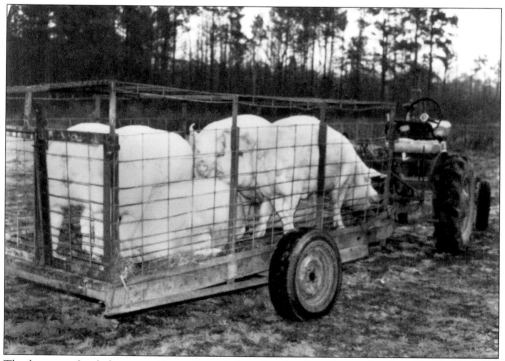

The hogs are loaded on a trailer and carried to the slaughter house. In the old days the hogs would be killed at the farm but now that job is done by professionals.

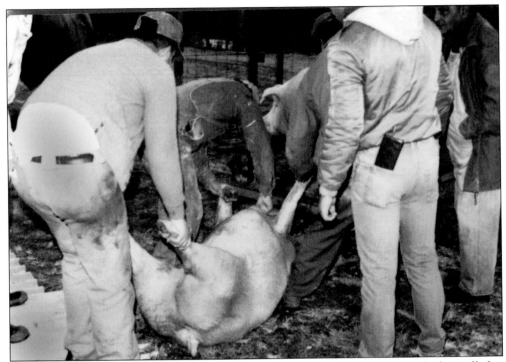

These people get the hog ready to go into the vat of boiling water. They scrape the hair off after it gets hot.

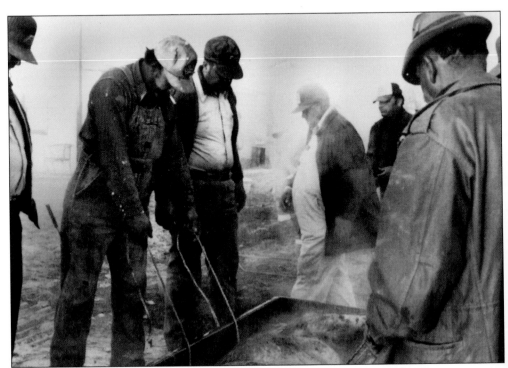

Those working must turn the hog in the vat to make sure that it is heated evenly.

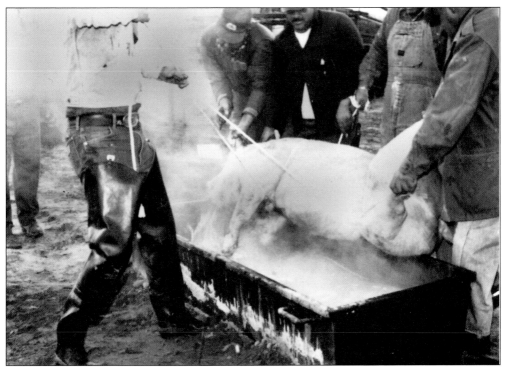

Here they lift the hog out of the vat. They will then hang the hog and then scrape the skin to remove the hair and rough skin.

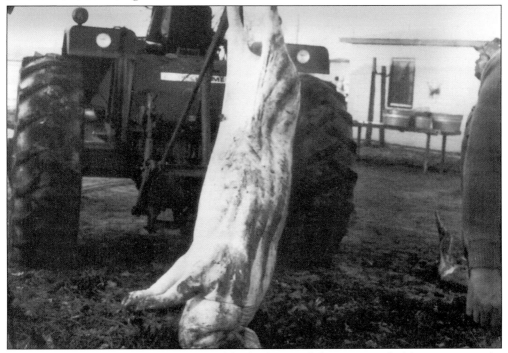

Hanging the hog also allowed the hog to bleed. They used the tractor to hold it up so it can be reached. Some people had high racks and used a block and tackle to raise and hold the hog.

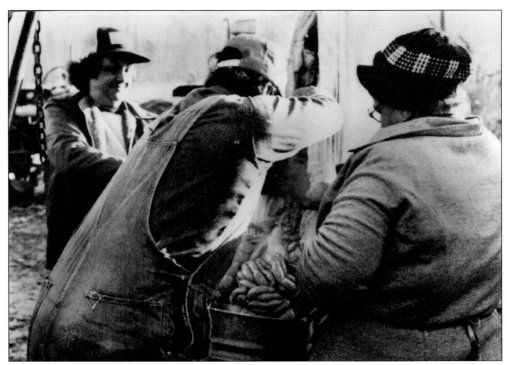

Next, the hog's entrails are cleaned out from the hog's cavity. All of these are used in some way or another. Liver pudding is made from the liver, lungs, and other organs. The intestines are cleaned out and used for casings.

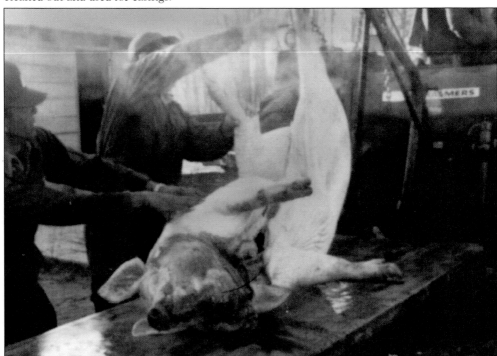

The cleaned-out hog is placed on a table to be cut up into serving-sized parts.

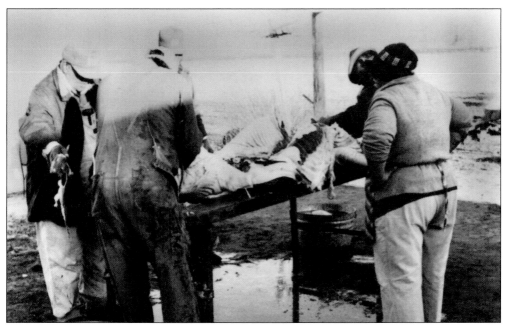

They cut off the hams, shoulders, and loins. They trim the fat off to make lard and also cook the skin to get out the fat. The skin and residue from the cooking-down of the lard is called cracklings and is used in cornbread.

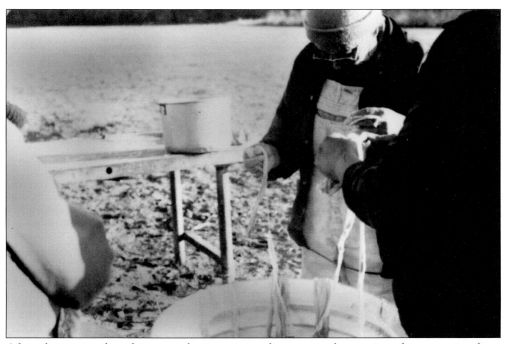

After cleaning and washing out the intestines, they are used as casings for sausage or liver pudding. They are heated in boiling water to completely sterilize them.

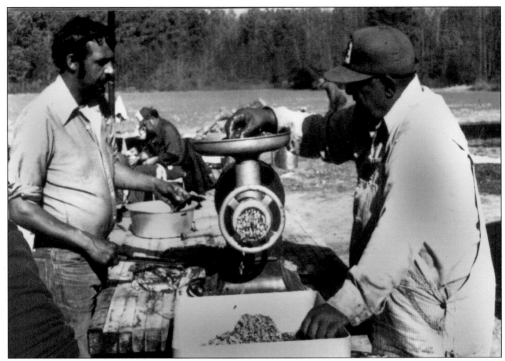

Here Hurbert and Martin Clark grind the meat to make sausage. The seasonings used in the sausage vary and each family had its favorite.

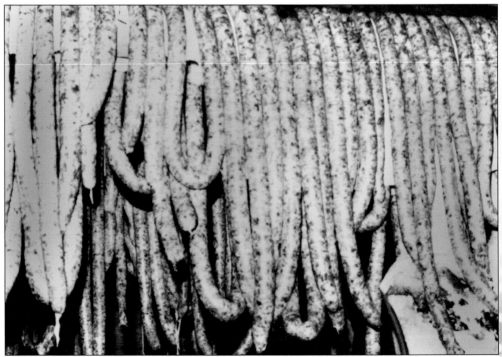

The sausage hangs after it has been stuffed in the casings. Some people cure the sausage by drying. The hams and shoulders are cured and hung in the smoke house.

Eight

LAURINBURG-MAXTON AIRBASE

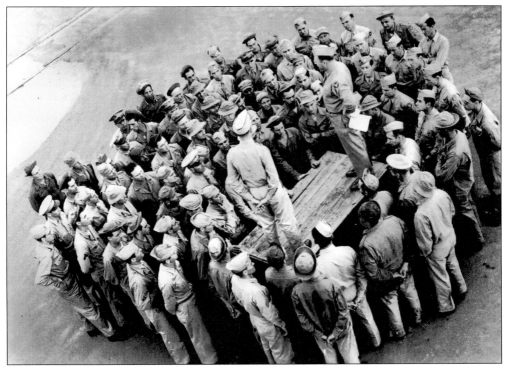

During World War II the Laurinburg-Maxton Air base was the training base for glider pilots. Here, the enlisted men of the Quartermaster Corps meet to hear the day's orders. Pictures in this chapter were collected by Maj. Rufus Pittman who was on the base throughout its entire operation. After the war, he was assigned to decommission the base. (Courtesy of Margaret Pittman.)

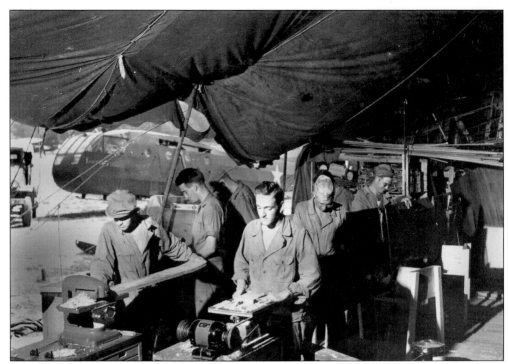

The glider tent was set up for construction of the gliders on the site. Here some men are building and setting up a glider. Some parts were built elsewhere and set up here, while other parts had to be made on the site.

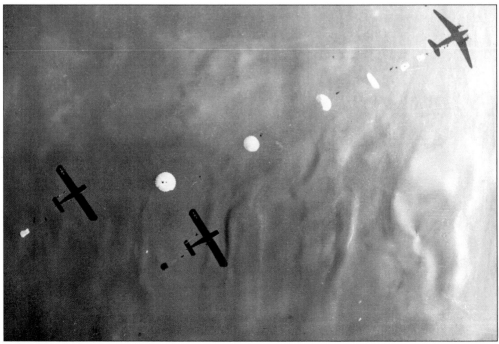

Paratroopers jumped from gliders to land behind enemy lines. Many of the pilots and crew members called them "flying coffins" because they were so dangerous.

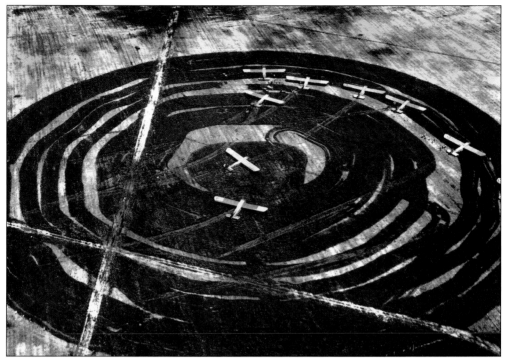

This picture, taken from an airplane, shows the air base while it was in operation. Note the circular patterns to the fields and the long runways. The base was one of the only places that had long enough runways on which early jets could land.

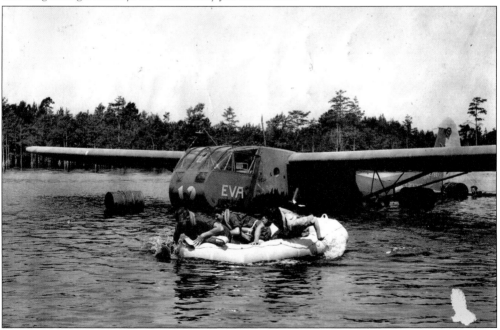

Glider pilots were trained in the local area. Here they learn what to do if they happened to land on water. The gliders were developed for the invasion of Europe; therefore landing in the ocean was certainly a possibility.

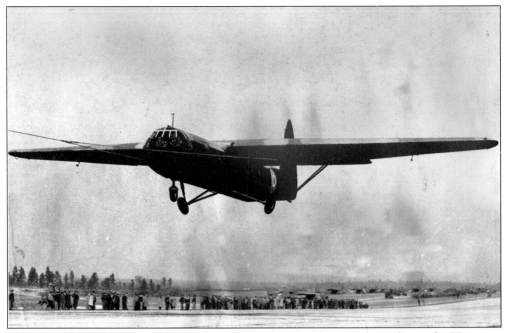

The crew of the glider would be inside with no way of adding power to their ride. However, they could steer the glider to catch updrafts and prolong their time in the air. Here, the glider is being pulled off the runway by an airplane at the airbase.

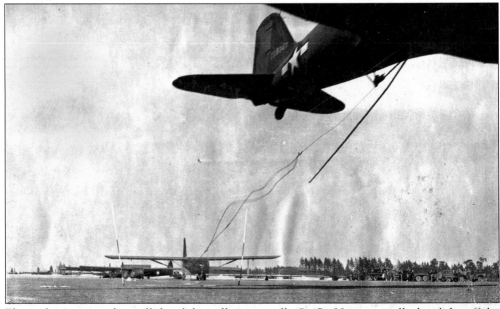

Planes that were used to pull the gliders off were usually C-47s. Here one pulls the glider off the runway. Some of the buildings and the land shown is now being used as an industrial park. The present airport on the site serves local individual pilots and industrial planes, and several large airplanes are mothballed there. The county still gets lots of use from this property.